NATURE'S FINER FORCES

NATURE'S FINER FORCES

(Translated from the Sanskrit with 15 Introductory & Explanatory
Essays on Nature's
Finer Forces)

BY

RAMA PRASAD

Ancient Wisdom Publication Woodland, California

ISBN: 978-1-963956-22-1

Contents

Preface

A word of explanation is necessary with regard to the book now offered to the public. In the 9th and 10th volumes of the theosophist I wrote certain Essays on "Nature's Finer Forces". The subject of these essays interested the readers of the Theosophist so much that I was asked to issue the series of Essays in book form. I found that in order to make a book they must be almost entirely rearranged, and perhaps rewritten. I was, however, not equal to the task of rewriting what I had once written. I therefore determined to publish a translation of the book in Sanskrit on the Science of the Breath and the Philosophy of the Tatwas. As, however, without these Essays the book would have been quite unintelligible, I decided to add them to the book by way of an illustrative introduction. This accordingly has been done. The Essays in the theosophist have been reprinted with certain additions, modifications, and corrections. Besides, I have written seven more Essays in order to make the explanations more complete and authoritative. Thus there are altogether 15 introductory and explanatory Essays.

I was confirmed in this course by one more consideration. The book contains a good deal more than the essays touched upon, and I thought it better to lay all of it before the public.

The book is sure to throw a good deal of light upon the scientific researches of the ancient Aryans of India, and it will leave no doubt in a candid mind that the religion of ancient India had a scientific basis. It is chiefly for this reason that I have drawn my illustrations of the Tatwic Law from the Upanishads.

There is a good deal in the book that can only be shown to be true by long and diligent experiment. Those who are devoted to the pursuit of truth without prejudice will no doubt be ready to wait before they form any opinion about such portions of the book. Others it is useless to reason with.

To the former class of students I have to say one word more. From my own experience I can tell them that the more they study the book, the more wisdom they are sure to find in it, and let me hope that ere long I shall have a goodly number of colleagues, who will with me try their best to explain and illustrate the book still better, and more thoroughly.

Rama Prasad
Merut (India)
5 November 1889

I. The Tatwas

The tatwas are the five modifications of the great Breath. Acting upon prakriti, this Great breath throws it into five states, having distinct vibratory motions, and performing different functions. The first outcome of the Evolutionary State of parabrahma is the akasa tatwa. After this come in order the vayu, the taijas, the apas and the prithivi. They are variously known as mahabhutas. The word akasa is generally translated into English by the word ether. Unfortunately, however, sound is not known to be the distinguishing quality of ether in modern English Science. Some few might also have the idea that the modern medium of light is the same as akasa. This, I believe, is a mistake. The luminiferous ether is the subtle taijas tatwa, and not the akasa. All the five subtle tatwas might no doubt be called ethers, but to use it for the word akasa, without any distinguishing epithet, is misleading. We might call akasa the sonoriferous ether, the vayu the tangiferous ether, apas the gustiferous ether, and prithivi the odoriferous ether. Just as there exists in the universe the luminiferous ether, an element of refined mater without which it has been found that the phenomena of light find no adequate explanation, so do there exist the four remaining ethers, elements of refined matter, without which it will be found that the phenomena of sound, touch, taste and smell find no adequate explanation.

The luminiferous ether is supposed by Modern Science to be Matter in a most refined state. It is the vibrations of this element that are said to constitute light. The vibrations are said to take place at right angles to the direction of the wave. Nearly the same is the description of the taijas tatwa given in the book. It makes this tatwa move in an upward direction, and the center of the direction is, of course, the direction of the wave. Besides, it says that one whole vibration of this element makes the figure of a triangle.

Suppose in the figure:

AB is the direction of the wave; BC is the direction of the vibration. CA is the line along which, seeing that in expansion the symmetrical arrangements of the atoms of a body are not changed, the vibrating atom must return to its symmetrical position in the line AB.

The taijas tatwa of the Ancients is then exactly the luminiferous ether of the Moderns, so far as the nature of the vibration is concerned. There is no exception, however, of the four remaining ethers, at all events in a direct manner, in Modern Science. The vibrations of akasa, the soniferous ether, constitute sound; and it is quite necessary to recognize the distinctive character of this form of motion.

The experiment of the bell in a vacuum goes to prove that the vibrations of atmosphere propagate sound. Any other media, however, such as the earth and the metals, are known to transmit sound in various degrees. There must, therefore, be some one thing in all these media which gives birth to sound – the vibration that constitutes sound. That something is the Indian akasa.

But akasa is all-pervading, just as the luminiferous ether. Why, then, is not sound transmitted to our ears when a vacuum is produced in the bell-jar? The real fact is that we must make a difference between the vibrations of the elements that constitute sound and light, etc., and the vibrations in the media which transmit these impressions to our senses.

It is not the vibrations of the ethers – the subtle tatwas – that cause our perceptions, but the ethereal vibrations transferred to different media, which are so many modifications of gross matter – the sthula Mahabhutas. The luminiferous ether is present just as much in a darkened room as in the space without. The minutest space within the dimensions of the surrounding walls themselves is not void of it. For all this the luminosity of the exterior is not present in the interior. Why? The reason is that our ordinary vision does not see the vibrations of the luminiferous ether. It only sees the vibrations of the media that the ether pervades. The capability of being set into ethereal vibrations varies with different media. In the space without the darkened room the ether brings the atoms of the atmosphere into the necessary state of visual vibration, and one wide expanse of light is presented to our view. The same is the case with every other object that we see. The ether that pervades the object brings the atoms of that object into the necessary state of visual vibration. The strength of the ethereal vibrations that the presence of the sun imparts to the ether pervading our planet is not sufficient to evoke the same state in the dead matter of the darkening walls. The internal ether, divided from the eternal one by this dead mass, is itself cut off from such vibrations. The darkness of the room is thus the consequence, notwithstanding the presence therein of the luminiferous ether. An electric spark in the vacuum of a bell-jar must needs be transmitted to our eyes, because the glass of the jar which stands in contact with the internal luminiferous ether has a good deal of the quality of being put into the state of visual vibration, which from thence is transmitted to the external ether and thence to the eye. The same would never be the case if we were to use a porcelain or an earthen jar. It is this capability of being put into the state of visual vibrations that we call transparency in glass and similar objects.

To return to the soniferous ether (akasa): Every form of gross matter has, to a certain extent, which varies with various forms, what we may call auditory transparency.

Now I have to say something about the nature of the vibrations. Two things must be understood in this connection. In the first place the external form of the vibration is something like the hole of the ear:

It throws matter which is subject to it, into the form of a dotted sheet:

These dots are little points, rising above the common surface so as to produce microscopic pits in the sheet. It is said to move by fits and starts (sankrama), and to move in all directions (sarvatogame). It means to say that the impulse falls back upon itself along the line of its former path, which lies on all sides of the direction of the wave:

It will be understood that these ethers produce in gross media vibrations similar to their own. The form, therefore, into which the auditory vibrations throw the atmospheric air is a true clue to the form of the ethereal vibration. And the vibrations of atmospheric air discovered by Modern Science are similar.

Now we come to the tangiferous ether (vayu). The vibrations of this ether are described as being spherical in form, and the motion is said to be at acute angles to the wave (tiryak). Such is the representation of these vibrations on the plane of the paper:

The remarks about the transmission of sound in the case of akasa apply here too, mutatis mutandis. The gustiferous ether (apas tatwa) is said to resemble in shape the half moon. It is, moreover, said to move downward. This direction is opposite to that of the luminiferous ether. This force therefore causes contraction. Here is the representation of the apas vibrations on the plane of paper:

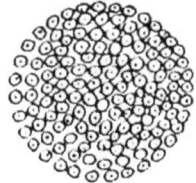

The process of contraction will be considered when I come to the qualities of the tatwas. The odoriferous ether (prithivi) is said to be quadrangular in shape, thus:

This is said to move in the middle. It neither moves at right angles, nor at acute angles, nor upwards, nor downwards, but it moves along the line of the wave. The line and the quadrangle are in the same plane.

These are the forms, and the modes of motion, of the five ethers.

Of the five sensations of men, each of these gives birth to one, thus:

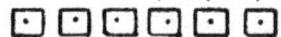

(1) Akasa, Sonorifierous ether, Sound; (2) Vayu, Tangiferous ether, Touch; (3) Taijas, Luminfierous ether, Color; (4) Apas, Gustiferous ether, Taste; (5) Prithivi, Odoriferous ether, Smell.

In the process of evolution, these co-existing ethers, while retaining their general, relative forms and primary qualities, contract the qualities of the other tatwas. This is known as the process of panchikarana, or division into five.

If we take, as our book does, H, P, R, V and L to be the algebraic symbols for (1), (2), (3), (4), and (5), respectively, after panchikarana the ethers assume the following forms:

One molecule of each ether, consisting of eight atoms, has four of the original principle ethers, and one of the remaining four.

The following table will show the five qualities of each of the tatwas after panchikarana: Sound Touch Taste Color Smell

	H	P	R	V	L
(1) H=	— +	— +	— +	— +	—
	2	8	8	8	8

	P	H	R	V	L
(2) P=	— +	— +	— +	— +	—
	2	8	8	8	8

	R	H	P	V	L
(3) R=	— +	— +	— +	— +	—
	2	8	8	8	8

	V	R	H	P	L
(4) V=	— +	— +	— +	— +	—
	2	8	8	8	8

	L	V	R	H	P
(5) L=	— +	— +	— +	— +	—
	2	8	8	8	8

(1) H ordinary ... ...
(2) P very light cool acid light blue acid
(3) R light very hot hot red hot
(4) V heavy cool astringent white astringent
(5) L deep warm sweet yellow sweet

It might be remarked here that the subtle tatwas exist now in the universe on four planes. The higher of these planes differ from the lower in having a greater number of vibrations per second. The four planes are:

(1) Physical (Prana); (2) Mental (Manas); (3) Psychic (Vijnana); (4) Spiritual (Ananda) I shall discuss, however, some of the secondary qualities of these tatwas.

(1) Space ~ This is a quality of the akasa tatwa. It has been asserted that the vibration of this ether is shaped like the hole of the ear, and that in the body thereof are microscopic points (vindus). It follows evidently that the interstices between the points serve to give space to ethereal minima, and offer them room for locomotion (avakasa).

(2) Locomotion ~ This is the quality of the vayu tatwa. Vayu is a form of motion itself, for motion in all directions is motion in a circle, large or small. The vayu tatwa itself has the form of spherical motion. When to the motion which keeps the form of the different ethers is added to the

stereotyped motion of the vayu, locomotion is the result.

(3) Expansion ~ This is the quality of the taijas tatwa. This follows evidently from the shape and form of motion which is given to this ethereal vibration. Suppose ABC is a lump of metal:

If we apply fire to it, the luminiferous ether in it is set in motion, and that drives the gross atoms of the lump into similar motion. Suppose (a) is an atom. This being impelled to assume the shape of the taijas, vibration goes towards (a'), and then takes the symmetrical position of (a"). Similarly does every point change its place round the center of the piece of metal. Ultimately the whole piece assumes the shape of A'B'C'. Expansion is thus the result.

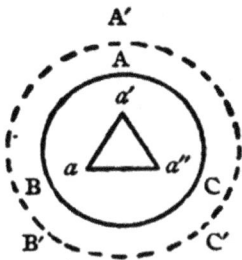

(4) Contraction ~ This is the quality of the apas tatwa. As has been remarked before, the direction of this ether is the reverse of the agni, and it is therefore easy to understand that contraction is the result of the play of this tatwa.

(5) Cohesion ~ This is the quality of the prithivi tatwa. It will be seen that this is the reverse of akasa. Akasa gives room for locomotion, while prithivi resists it. This is the natural result of the direction and shape of this vibration. It covers up the spaces of the akasa.

(6) Smoothness ~ This is a quality of the apas tatwa. As the atoms of any body in contraction come near each other and assume the semi-lunar shape of the apas, they must easily glide over each other. The very shape secures easy motion for the atoms.

This, I believe, is sufficient to explain the general nature of the tatwas. The different phases of their manifestation on all the planes of life will be taken up in their proper places.

II. Evolution

It will be very interesting to trace the development of man and the development of the world according to the theory of the tatwas.

The tatwas, as we have already seen, are the modifications of Swara. Regarding Swara, we find in our book: "In the Swara are the Vedas and the shastras, and in the Swara is music. All the world is in the Swara; Swara is the spirit itself." The proper translation of the word Swara is "the current of the life-wave". It is that wavy motion which is the cause of the evolution of cosmic undifferentiated matter into the differentiated universe, and the involution of this into the primary state of non-differentiation, and so on, in and out, forever and ever. From whence does this motion come? This motion is the spirit itself. The word atma used in the book, itself carries the idea of eternal motion, coming as it does from the root at, eternal motion; and it may be significantly remarked, that the root at is connected with (and in fact is simply another form of) the roots ah, breath, and as, being. All these roots have for their original the sound produced by the breathing of animals. In The Science of Breath the symbol for inspiration is sa, and for expiration ha. It is easy to see how these symbols are connected with the roots as and ah. The current of life-wave spoken of above is technically called Hansachasa, i.e., the motion of ha and sa. The word Hansa, which is taken to mean God, and is made so much of in many Sanskrit works, is only the symbolic representation of the eternal processes of life – ha and sa.

The primeval current of life-wave is, then, the same which in man assumes the form of inspiratory and expiratory motion of the lungs, and this is the all-pervading source of the evolution and the involution of the universe.

The book goes on: "It is the Swara that has given form to the first accumulations of the divisions of the universe; the Swara causes involution and evolution; the Swara is God Himself, or more properly the great Power (Mahashwara)." The Swara is the manifestation of the impression on matter of that power which in man is known to us as the power that knows itself. It is to be understood that the action of this power never ceases. It is ever at work, and evolution and involution are the very necessity of its unchangeable existence.

The Swara has two different states. The one is known on the physical plane as the sun- breath, the other as the moon-breath. I shall, however, at the present stage of evolution designate them as positive and negative respectively. The period during which this current comes back to the point from whence it started is known as the night of parabrahma. The positive or evolutionary period is known as the day of parabrahma; the negative or involutionary portion is known as the night of parabrahma. These nights and days follow each other without break. The sub-divisions of this period comprehend all the phases of existence, and it is therefore necessary to give her the scale of time according to the Hindu Shastras.

The Divisions of Time

I shall begin with a Truti as the least division of time.
26-2/3 truti = 1 nimesha = 8/45 second.
18 nimesha = 1 kashtha = 3-1/5 seconds = 8 vipala.
30 kashtha = 1 kala = 1-3/5 minutes = 4 pala.
30 kala = 1 mahurta = 48 minutes = 2 ghari.
30 mahurta = 1 day and night = 24 hours = 60 ghari.
30 days and nights and odd hours = 1 Pitruja day
 and night = 1 month and odd hours.
12 months = 1 Daiva day and night = 1 year = 365 days, 15", 30", 31".
365 Daiva days and nights = 1 Daiva year.
4,800 Daiva years = 1 Satya yuga.
3,600 Daiva years = 1 Treta yuga.
2,400 Daiva years = 1 Dwapara yuga.
1,200 Daiva years = 1 Kali yuga.
12,000 Daiva years = 1 Chaturyugi (four yuga).
12,000 Chaturyugi = 1 Daiva yuga.
2,000 Daiva yuga = 1 day and night of Brahma.
365 Brahmic days and nights = 1 year of Brahma.
71 Daiva yuga = 1 Manwantara.
12,000 Brahmic years = 1 Chaturyuga of Brahma, and so one.
200 yuga of Brahma = 1 day and night of parabrahma.

These days and nights follow each other in eternal succession, and hence eternal evolution and involution.

We have thus five sets of days and night: (1) Parabrahma, (2) Brahma, (3) Daiva, (4) Pitrya, (5) Manusha. A sixth is the Manwantara day, and the Manwantara night (pralaya).

The days and nights of parabrahma follow each other without beginning or end. The night (the negative period and the day (the positive period) both merge into the susumna (the conjunctive period) and merge into each other. And so do the other days and nights. The days all through this division are sacred to the positive, the hotter current, and the nights are sacred to the negative, the cooler current. The impressions of names and forms, and the power of producing an impression, lie in the positive phase of existence. Receptivity is given birth to by the negative current.

After being subjected to the negative phase of parabrahma, Prakriti, which follows parabrahma like a shadow, has been saturated with evolutionary receptivity; as the hotter current sets in, changes are imprinted upon it, and it appears in changed forms. The first imprint that the evolutionary positive current leaves upon Prakriti is known as akasa. Then, by and by the remaining ethers come into existence. These modifications of Prakriti are the ethers of the first stage.

Into these five ethers, as now constituting the objective phase, works on the current of the Great Breath. A further development takes place. Different centers come into existence. The akasa throws them into a form that gives room for locomotion. With the beginning of the vayu tatwa these elementary ethers are thrown into the form of spheres. This was the beginning of formation, or what may also be called solidification.

These spheres are our Brahmandas. In them the ethers assume a secondary development. The so-called division into five takes place. In this Brahmic sphere in which the new ethers have good room for locomotion, the taijas tatwa now comes into play, and then the apas tatwa. Every tatwic quality is generated into, and preserved in, these spheres by these currents. In process of time we have a center and an atmosphere. This sphere is the self- conscious universe.

In this sphere, according to the same process, a third ethereal state comes into existence. In the cooler atmosphere removed from the center another class of centers comes into existence. These divide the Brahmic state of matter into two different states. After this comes into existence another state of matter whose centers bear the names of devas or suns.

We have thus four states of subtle matter in the universe:

(1) Prana, life matter, with the sun for center; (2) Manas, mental matter, with the manu for center; (3) Vijnana, psychic matter, with Brahma for center; (4) Ananda, spiritual matter, with parabrahma as the infinite substratum.

Every higher state is positive with regard to the lower one, and every lower on is given birth to by a combination of the positive and negative phase of the higher.

(1) Prana has to do with three sets of days and nights in the above division of time: (a) Our ordinary days and nights; (b) The bright and dark half of the month which are called the pitrya day and night; (c) The northern and southern halves of the years, the day and night of the devas.

These three nights acting upon earth-matter impart to it the receptivity of the cool, negative shady phase of life-matter. These nights imprint themselves on the respective days coming in after it. The earth herself thus becomes a living being, having a north pole, in which a central force draws the needle towards itself, and a south pole in which is centered a for which is, so to speak, the shade of the north polar center. It has also always a solar force centered in the eastern half, and the lunar -- the shade of the former – centered in the western half.

These centers come, in fact, into existence even before the earth is manifested on the gross plane. So too do the centers of other planets come into existence. As the sun presents himself to the manu there come into existence two states of matter in which the sun lives and moves – the positive and the negative. As the solar prana, after having been for some time subjected to the negative shady state, is subjected in its revolutionary course to the source of its positive phase, manu, the figure of manu is imprinted upon it. This manu is, in fact, the universal mind, and all the planets with their inhabitants are the phases of his existence. Of this, however, more heareafter. At present we see that earth-life or Terrestrial Prana has four centers of force.

When it has been cooled by the negative current, the positive phase imprints itself upon it, and earth-life in various forms comes into existence. The essays on prana will explain this more clearly.

(2) Manas: this has to do with manu. The suns revolve round these centers with the whole of their atmospheres of prana. This system gives birth to the lokas or spheres of life, of which the planets are one class.

These lokas have been enumerated by Vyasa in his commentary on the Yogasutra (III. Pada, 26th Sutra). The aphorism runs thus:

"By meditation upon the sun is obtained a knowledge of the physical creation."
On this, the revered commentator says: "There are seven lokas (spheres of existence)." (1) The Bhurloka: this extends to the Meru; (2) Antareikshaloka: this extends from the surface of the Meru to the Dhru,

the pole-star, and contains the planets, the nakstatras, and the stars; (3) Beyond that is the swarloka: this is fivefold and sacred to Mahendra; (4) Maharloka: This is sacred to the Prajapati; (5) Janaloka; (6) Tapas loka, and; (7) Satya loka. These three (5, 6, and 7) are sacred to Brahma.

It is not my purpose to try at present to explain the meaning of these lokas. It is sufficient for my present purpose to say that the planets, the stars, the lunar mansions are all impressions of manu, just as the organisms of the earth are the impressions of the sun. The solar prana is prepared for this impression during the manwantara night.

Similarly, Vijnana has to do with the nights and days of Brahma, and Ananda with those of Parabrahma.

It will thus be seen that the whole process of creation, on whatever plane of life, is performed most naturally by the five tatwas in their double modifications, the positive and negative. There is nothing in the universe that the Universal Tatwic Law of Breath does not comprehend.

After this brief exposition of the theory of tatwic evolution comes a series of Essays, taking up all the subtle states of matter one by one, and describing more in detail the working of the tatwic law in those planes, and also the manifestations of these planes of life in humanity.

III. *The Mutual Relation of the Tatwas and of the Principles*

The akasa is the most important of all the tatwas. It must, as a matter of course, precede and follow every change of state on every plane of life. Without this there can be no manifestation or cessation of forms. It is out of akasa that every form comes, and it is in akasa that every form lives. The akasa is full of forms in their potential state. It intervenes between every two of the five tatwas, and between every two of the five principles.

The evolution of the tatwas is always part of the evolution of a certain definite form. Thus the manifestation of the primary tatwas is with the definite aim of giving what we may call a body, a Prakritic form to the Iswara. In the bosom of the Infinite Parabrahma, there are hidden unnumerable such centers. One center takes under its influence a certain portion of the Infinite, and there we find first of all coming into existence the akasa tatwa. The extent of this akasa limits the extent of the Universe, and out of it the Iswara is to come. With this end comes out of this akasa the Vayu tatwa. This pervades the whole Universe and has a certain center that serves to keep the whole expanse together, and separate as one whole, from other universes (Brahmandas).

It has been mentioned, and further on will be more clearly explained, that every tatwa has a positive and a negative phase. It is also evident on the analogy of the sun that places more distant from the center are always negative to those which are nearer. We might say that they are cooler than these, as it will be seen later on the heat is not peculiar to the sun only, but that all the higher centers have a greater amount of heat than even the sun itself.

Well then, in this Brahmic sphere of Vayu, except for some space near the parabrahmic akasa, every atom of the vayu is reacted upon by an opposite force. The more distant and therefore the cooler one reacts upon the nearer and therefore the hotter. The equal and opposite vibrations of the same force cancel each other, and both together pass into the akasic state. Thus, while some of this space remains filled up by the Brahmic Vayu on account of the constant outflow of this tatwa from the parabrahmic akasa, the remainder is rapidly turned into akasa. This akasa is the mother of the Brahmic agni tatwa. The agni tatwa working similarly gives birth through another akasa to the apas, and this similarly to the prithivi. This Brahmic prithivi thus contains the qualities of all the preceding tatwas besides a fifth one of its own.

The first stage of the Universe, the ocean of psychic matter has now come into existence in its entirety. This matter is, of course, very, very fine, and there is absolutely no grossness in it as compared with the matter of the fifth plane. In this ocean shines the intelligence of Iswara, and this ocean, with everything that might be manifest in it, is the self-conscious universe.

In this psychic ocean, as before, the more distant atoms are negative to the nearer ones. Hence, except a certain space which remains filled with the psychic prithivi on account of the constant supply of this element from above, the rest begins to change into an akasa. This second akasa is full of what are called Manus in their potential state. The Manus are so many groups of certain mental forms, the ideals of the various genera and species of life to appear further on. We have to do with one of these.

Impelled by the evolutionary current of the Great Breath, manu comes out of this akasa, in the same way as Brahma did out of the parabrahmic akasa. First and uppermost in the mental sphere is the Vayu, and then in regular order the taijas, the apas, and the prithivi. This mental matter follows the same laws, and similarly begins to pass into the third akasic state, which is full of innumerable suns. They come out in the same way, and begin to work on a similar plan, which will be better understood here than higher up.

Everybody can test here for himself that the more distant portions of the solar system are cooler than the nearer ones. Every little atom of Prana is comparatively cooler than the adjacent one towards the sun from itself. Hence equal and opposite vibrations cancel each other. Leaving, therefore, a certain space near the sun as always filled up with the tatwas of Prana, which are there being constantly supplied from the sun, the rest of the Prana passes into the akasic state.

It might be noted down here that the whole of this Prana is made up of innumerable little points. In the future I shall speak of these points of as trutis, and might say here that it is these trutis that appear on the terrestrial plane as atoms (anu or paramanu). They might be spoken of as solar atoms. These solar atoms are of various classes according to the prevalence of one or more of the constituent tatwas.

Every point of Prana is a perfect picture of the whole ocean. Every other point is represented in every point. Every atom has, therefore, for its constituents, all the four tatwas, in varying proportions according to its position in respect of others. The different classes of these solar atoms appear on the terrestrial plane as the various elements of chemistry.

The spectrum of every terrestrial element reveals the color or colors of the prevalent tatwa or tatwas of a solar atom of that substance. The greater the heat to which any substance is subjected the nearer does the element approaches its solar state. Heat destroys for the time being the terrestrial coatings of the solar atoms.

The spectrum of sodium thus shows the presence of the yellow prithivi, that of lithium, the red agni and the yellow prithivi, that of cesium, the red agni, the green admixture, the yellow prithivi, and the blue vayu. Rubidium shows red, orange, yellow, green and blue, i.e., the agni, prithivi and agni, prithivi, vayu and prithivi, and vayu. These classes of solar atoms that make up all put altogether, the wide expanse of the solar prana, pass into the akasic state. While the sun keeps up a constant supply of these atoms, those that are passing into the akasic state pass on the other side into the planetary vayu. Certain measured portions of the solar akasa naturally separate themselves from others, according to the differing creation that is to appear in those portions. These portions of akasa are called lokas. The earth itself is a loka called the Bhurloka. I shall take up the earth for further illustration of the law.

That portion of the solar akasa that is the immediate mother of the Earth, first gives birth to the terrestrial Vayu. Every element is now in the state of the Vayu tatwa, which may now be called gaseous. The Vayu tatwa is spherical in shape, and thus the gaseous planet bears similar outlines. The center of this gaseous sphere keeps together round itself the whole expanse of gas. As soon as this gaseous sphere comes into existence, it is subjected to the following influences among others:

(1) The superposed influence of the solar heat; (2) The internal influence of the more distant atoms on the nearer ones and vice versa.

The first influence has a double effect upon the gaseous sphere. It imparts more heat to the nearer hemisphere than to the more distant one. The superficial air of the nearer hemisphere having contracted a certain amount of solar energy, rises towards the sun. Cooler air from below takes its place. But where does the superficial air go? It cannot pass beyond the limit of the terrestrial sphere, which is surrounded by the solar akasa through which comes a supply from the solar Prana. It therefore begins to move in a circle, and thus a rotary motion is established in the sphere. This is the origin of the earth's rotation upon its axis.

Again, as a certain amount of the solar energy is imparted to the gaseous terrestrial sphere, the impulse of the upward motion reaches the center itself. Therefore that center itself, and along with it the whole sphere, moves towards the sun. It cannot, however, go on in this direction, for a nearer approach would destroy that balance of forces that gives the earth its peculiarities. A loka that is nearer to the sun than our planet cannot have the same conditions of life. Hence, while the sun draws the earth towards itself, those laws of life that have given it a constitution, on which ages must roll on, keep it in the sphere they have assigned to it. Two forces thus come into existence. Drawn by one the earth would go towards the sun; checked by the other it must remain where it is. These are the centrifugal and the centripetal forces, and their action results in giving the earth its annual revolution.

Secondly, the internal action of the gaseous atoms upon each other ends in the change of the whole gaseous sphere, except the upper portion, into the akasic state. This akasic state gives birth to the igneous (pertaining to the agni tatwa) state of terrestrial matter. This changes similarly into the apas, and this again into the prithivi.

The same process obtains in the changes of matter with which we are now familiar. An example will better illustrate the whole law.

Take ice. This is solid, or what the Science of Breath would call in the state of prithivi. One quality of the prithivi tatwa, the reader will remember, is cohesive resistance. Let us apply heat to this ice. As this heat passes into the ice, it is indicated by the thermometer. When the temperature rises to 78 degrees, the ice changes its state. But the thermometer no longer indicates the same amount of heat. 78 degrees of heat have become latent.

Let us now apply 536 degrees of heat to a pound of boiling water. As is generally known, this great quantity of heat becomes latent while the water passes into the gaseous state.

Now let us follow the reverse process. To gaseous water let us apply a certain amount of cold. When this cold becomes sufficient entirely to counteract the heat that keeps it in the gaseous state, the vapor passes into the akasa state, and from thence into the taijas state. It is not necessary that the whole of the vapor should at once pass into the next state. The change is gradual. As the cold is gradually passing into the vapor, the taijas modification is gradually appearing out of, and through the intervention of akasa, into which it had passed during latency. This is being indicated on the thermometer. When the whole has passed into the igneous state, and the thermometer has indicated 536 degrees, the second akasa comes into existence. Out of this second akasa comes the liquid state at the same temperature, the whole heat having again passed into the akasa state, and therefore no longer indicated by the thermometer.

When cold is applied to this liquid, heat again begins to come out, and when it reaches 78 degrees, this heat having come out of and through the akasa, into which it had passed, the whole liquid had passed into the igneous state. Here it again begins to pass into the akasa state. The thermometer begins to fall down, and out of this akasa begins to come the prithivi state of water --- ice.

Thus we see that the heat which is given out by the influence of cold passes into the akasa state, which becomes the substratum of a higher phase, and the heat which is absorbed passes into another akasa state, which becomes the substratum of a lower phase.

It is in this way that the terrestrial gaseous sphere changes into its present state. The experiment described above points out many important truths about the relation of these tatwas to each other.

First of all it explains that very important assertion of the Science of Breath which says that every succeeding tatwic state has the qualities of all the foregoing tatwic states. Thus we see that as the gaseous state of water is being acted upon by cold, the latent heat of steam is being cancelled and passing into the akasa state. This cannot but be the case, since equal and opposite vibrations of the same force always cancel each other, and the result is the akasa. Out of this comes the taijas state of matter. This is that state in which the latent heat of steam becomes patent. It will be observed that this state has no permanence. The taijas form of water, as indeed any other substance, cannot exist for any length of time, because the major part of terrestrial matter is in the lower and therefore more negative states of apas and prithivi, and whenever for any cause any substance passes into the taijas state, the surrounding objects begin at once to react upon it with such force as at once to force it into the next akasa state. Those things that now live in the normal state of the apas or the prithivi find it quite against the laws of their existence to remain, except under external influence, in the taijas (igneous) state. Thus an atom of gaseous water before passing into the liquid state has already remained in the three states, the akasa, the gaseous, and the taijas. It must, therefore, have all the qualities of the three tatwas, and so it no doubt has. Cohesive resistance is only wanted, and that is the quality of the prithivi tatwa.

Now when this atom of liquid water passes into the icy state, what do we see? All the states that have preceded must again show themselves. Cold will cancel the latent heat of the liquid state, and the akasa state will come out. Out of this akasa state is sure to come the gaseous state. This gaseous (Vayava) state is evidenced by the gyrations and other motions that are set up in the body of the liquid by the mere application of the cold. The motion, however, is not of very long duration, and as they are ceasing (passing into the akasa state) the taijas state is coming out. This too, however, is not of long duration, and as this is passing into the akasa state, the ice is coming into existence.

It will be easy to see that all four states of terrestrial matter exist in our sphere. The gaseous (Vayava) is there in what we call the atmosphere; the igneous (taijas) is the normal temperature of earth life; the liquid (apas) is the ocean; the solid (prithivi) is the terra firma. None of these states, however, exists quite isolated from the other. Each is constantly invading the domain of the other, and thus it is difficult to find any portion of space filled up only with matter in one state. The two adjacent tatwas are found intermixed with each other to a greater degree than those that are removed from each other by an intermediate state. Thus prithivi will be found mixed up to a greater extent with water than with agni and vayu, apas with agni than with vayu, and vayu with agni more than with any other. It would thus appear from the above, according to the science of tatwas, that the flame and other luminous bodies on earth are not in the terrestrial taijas (igneous) state. They are in or near the solar state of matter.

IV. Prana (I)

The Centers of Prana; The Nadis; The Tatwic Centers of Life; The Ordinary Change of Breath

Prana, as already expressed, is that state of Tatwic matter which surrounds the sun, and in which moves the earth and other planets. It is the state next higher than matter in the terrestrial state. The terrestrial sphere is separated from the solar Prana by an akasa. Thisakasa is the immediate mother of the terrestrial vayu whose native color is blue. It is on this account that the sky looks blue.

Although at this point in the heavens, the Prana changes into akasa, which gives birth to the terrestrial Vayu, the rays of the sun that fall on the sphere from without are not stopped in their inward journey. They are refracted, but move onwards into the terrestrial sphere all the same. Through these rays the ocean of Prana, which surrounds our sphere, exerts upon it an organizing influence.

The terrestrial Prana – the earth-life that appears in the shape of all the living organisms of our planet – is, as a whole, nothing more than a modification of the solar Prana.

As the earth moves round her own axis and round the sun, twofold centers are developed in the terrestrial Prana. During the diurnal rotation every place, as it is subjected to the direct influence of the sun, sends forth the positive life-current from the East to the West. During the night the same place sends forth the negative current.

In the annual course the positive current travels from the North to the South during the six months of summer – the day of the devas – and the negative during the remaining six months – the night of the devas.

The North and East are thus sacred to the positive current; the opposite quarters to the negative current. The sun is the lord of the positive current, the moon of the negative, because the negative solar prana comes during the night to the earth from the moon.

The terrestrial prana is thus an ethereal being with double centers of work. The first is the northern, the second the southern. The two halves of these centers are the eastern and western centers. During the six months of summer the current of life runs from the North to the South, and during the months of winter the negative current goes the other way.

With every month, with every day, with every nimesha this current completes a minor course, and while this current continues in this course the diurnal rotation gives it an eastern or western direction. The northern current runs during the day of man from East to West, and during the night from West to East. The directions of the other current are respectively opposite to the above. So practically there are only two directions – the eastern and western. The difference of the northern and southern currents is not practically felt in terrestrial life. These two currents produce in the terrestrial prana two distinguishable modifications of the composing ethers. The rays of either of these ethereal modifications proceeding from their different centers run into each other – the one giving life, strength, form and other qualities to the other. Along the rays emerging from the northern center, run the currents of positive prana; along those emerging from the southern, the currents of negative prana. The eastern and western channels of these currents are respectively called Pingala and Ida, two of the celebrated nadis of the Tantrists. It will be better to discuss the other bearings of Prana, when we have localized it in the human body.

The influence of this terrestrial Prana develops two centers of work in the gross matter that is to form a human body. Part of the matter gathers round the northern, and part round the southern center. The northern center develops into the brain; the southern into the heart. The general shape of the terrestrial Prana is something like an ellipse. In this the northern focus is in the brain; the southern in the heart. The column along which the positive matter gathers runs between these foci.

The line in the middle is the place where the eastern and western – right and left – divisions of the column join. The column is the medulla oblongata the central line is also susumna, the right and left divisions the Pingala and Ida. The rays of Prana that diverge either way from these nadis are only their ramifications, and constitute together with them the nervous system.

The negative Prana gathers round the southern center. This, too, takes a form similar to the former. The right and left divisions of this column are the right and left divisions of the heart.

Each division has two principal ramifications, and each ramification again ramifies into others. The two openings either way are one a vein, and one an artery, the four opening into four chambers – the four petals of the lotus of the heart. The right part of the heart again, with all its ramifications, is called Pingala, the left Ida, and the middle part susumna.

There is reason to think, however, that the heart only is spoken of as the lotus, while the three foregoing names are set apart for the nervous system. The current of Prana works forward and backward, in and out. The cause of this lies in the momentary of the being of Prana. As the year advances, every moment a change of state takes place in the terrestrial prana, on account of the varying strengths of the solar and lunar currents. Thus, every moment is, strictly speaking, a new being of Prana. As Buddha says, all life is momentary. The Moment that is the first to throw into matter the germ that will develop the two centers is the first cause of organized life. If the succeeding Moments are friendly in their tatwic effect to the first cause, the organism gains strength and develops; if not, the impulse is rendered fruitless. The general effect of these succeeding moments keeps up general life; but the impulse of any one moment tends to pass off as the others come in. A system of forward and backward motion is thus established. One Moment of Prana proceeding from the center of work goes to the farthest ends of the gross vessels – nerves and blood vessels– of the organism. The succeeding moment gives it, however, the backwards impulse. A few moments are taken in the completion of the forward impulse, and the determination of the backward one. This period differs in different organisms. As the Prana runs forward, the lungs inspire; as it recedes, the process of expiration sets in.

The Prana moves in the Pingala when it moves from the northern center towards the east, and from the southern towards the west; it moves in Ida when it moves from the northern center towards the west, and from the southern center towards the east. This means that in the former case the Prana moves from the brain, towards the right, through the heart, to the left and back to the brain; and from the heart to the left through the brain to the right
back to the heart. In the latter the case is the reverse. To use other terms, in the former case the Prana moves from the nervous system to the right through the system of blood vessels to the left, and back again to the nervous system; or, from the system of blood vessels to the left through the nervous system to the right, and back again to the system of blood vessels. These two currents coincide. In the latter the case is the reverse. The left part of the body containing the nerves and the blood vessels may

be called Ida, the right the Pingala. The right and left bronchi form as well the part respectively of Pingala and Ida, as any other parts of the right and left divisions of the body. But what is susumna? One of the names of susumna is sandhi, the place where the two – Ida and Pingala – join. It is really that place from which the Prana may move either way – right or left – or, under certain circumstances, both ways. It is that place which the Prana must pass when it changes from the right to the left, and from the left to the right. It is therefore booth the spinal canal and the cardiac canal. The spinal canal extends from the Brahmarandhra, the northern center of Prana through the whole vertebral column (Brahmadanda).

The cardiac canal extends from the southern center midway between the two lobes of the heart. As the Prana moves from the spinal canal towards the right hand to the heart, the right lung works; the breath comes in and out of the right nostril. When it reaches the southern canal, you cannot feel the breath out of either nostril. As, however, it goes out of the cardiac canal to the left, the breath begins to come out of the left nostril, and flows through that until the Prana again reaches the spinal canal. There, again, you cease to feel the breath out of either nostril. The effect of these two positions of Prana is identical upon the flow of breath, and, therefore, I think that both the northern and southern canals are designated by susumna. If we may speak in this way, let us imagine that a plane passes midway between the spinal and cardiac canals. This plane will pass through the hollow of the susumna. But let it be understood that there is no such plane in reality. It will perhaps be more correct to say that as the rays of the positive Ida and Pingala spread either way as nerves, and those of the negative as blood-vessels, the rays of susumna spread all over the body midway between the nerves and blood vessels, the positive and negative nadis. The following is the description of susumna in the Science of Breath:

"When the breath goes in and out, one moment by the left and the other by the right nostril, that too is susumna. When Prana is in that nadi the fires of death burn; this is called vishuva. When it moves one moment in the right, and the other in the left, let it be called the Unequal State (vishamabhava); when it moves thorough both at once, the wise have called it vishuva...

"[It is susumna] at the time of the passing of the Prana from the Ida into the Pingala, or vice versa; and also of the change of one tatwa into another."

Then the susumna has two other functions. It is called vedo-veda in one of its manifestations, and sandhyasandhi in the other. As, however, the right and left directions of the cardiac Prana coincide with the left and right of the spinal current, there are some writers who dispense with the double susumna. According to them, the spinal canal alone is the susumna. The Uttaragita and Latachakra nirupana are works in this class. This method of explanation takes away a good deal of difficulty. The highest recommendation of this view is its comparative simplicity. The right side current from the heart, and the left side current from the spine may both be reckoned without difficulty as the left side spinal currents, and so may the remaining two currents be reckoned as the right side spinal currents.

One more consideration is in favor of this view. The nervous system represents the sun, the system of blood vessels the moon. Hence the real force of life dwells in the nerves. The positive and negative – the solar and lunar – phases of life matter are only different phases of Prana, the solar matter. The more distant and therefore the cooler matter is negative to the nearer, and therefore, the hotter. It is solar life that manifests itself in the various phases of the moon. To pass out of technicalities, it is nervous force that manifests itself in various forms, in the system of blood vessels. The blood vessels are only the receptacles of nervous force. Hence, in the nervous system, the real life of the gross body is the true Ida, Pingala and susumna. These are, in such a case, the spinal column, and the right and left sympathetics, with all their ramifications throughout the body.

The development of the two centers is thus the first stage in the development of the fetus. The matter that gathers up under the influence of the northern center is the spinal column; the matter that gathers up round the southern center is the heart. The diurnal rotation divides these columns or canals into the right and left divisions. Then the correlative influence of these two centers upon each other develops an upper and lower division in each of these centers. This happens somewhat in the same way, and on the same principle, as a Leyden jar is charged with positive electricity by a negative rod. Each of these centers is thus divided into four parts:

(1) The right side positive, (2) the left side positive, (3) the right side negative, and (4) the left side negative.

In the heart these four divisions are called the right and left auricles and ventricles. The Tantras style these four divisions the four petals of the cardiac lotus, and indicate them by various letters. The positive petals of the heart form the center from which proceed the positive blood vessels, the arteries; the negative petals are the starting points of the negative blood vessels, the veins. This negative prana is pregnant with ten forces:
(1) Prana, (2) Apana, (3) Samana, (4) Vyana, (5) Udana, (6) Krikila, (7) Naga, (8) Devadatta, (9) Dhavanjaya, (10) Kurma.

These ten forces are called vayu. The word vayu is derived from the root va, to move, and means nothing more than a motive power. The Tantrists do not mean to give it the idea of a gas. Henceforth I shall speak of the vayu as the forces or motive powers of prana. These ten manifestations of Prana are reduced by some writers to the first five alone, holding that the remaining ones are only modifications of the former, which are the all-important of the functions of prana. This, however, is only a question of division. From the left side positive petal the prana gathers up into a nadi that ramifies within the chest into the lungs, and again gathers up into a nadi that opens into the right side negative petal. This entire course forms something like a circle (chakra). This nadi is called in modern science the pulmonary artery and vein. Two lungs come into existence by the alternate workings of the positive and negative prana of the eastern and western powers.

Similarly, from the right side positive petal branch several nadi that go both upwards and downwards in two directions, the former under the influence of the northern, the latter under the influence of the southern powers. Both these nadi open after a circular march throughout the upper and lower portions of the body into the left side negative petal.

Between the left side positive and the right side negative petal is one chakra (disk). This chakra comprises the pulmonary artery, the lungs, and the pulmonary vein. The chest gives room to this chakra, which is positive with respect to the lower portions of the body, in which run the ramifications of the lower chakra, which latter joins the right side positive and the left side negative petals.

In the above chakra (in the cavity of the chest) is the seat of prana, the first and most important of the ten manifestations. Inspiration and expiration being a true index of the changes of prana, the pulmonary manifestations thereof have the same name. With the changes of prana we have a corresponding change in the other functions of life. The lower negative chakra contains the principal seats of some of the other manifestations of life. This apana is located in the long intestine, samana in the navel, and so on.

Also, udana is located in the throat; vyana all over the body. Udana causes belching; kurma in the eyes causes them to shut and open; krikila in the stomach causes hunger. In short, proceeding from the four petals of the heart we have an entire network of these blood vessels. There are two sets of these blood vessels side by side in every part of the body, connected by innumerable little channels, the capillaries.

We read in the Prasnopnisat:

"From the heart [ramify the] nadi. Of these there are 101 principal ones (Pradhana nadi). Each of these branches into 100. Each of these again into 72,000."

Thus, there are 10,100 branch nadi, and 727,200,000 still smaller ones, or what are called twig-nadi. The terminology is imitated from a tree. There is the root in the heart. From these proceed various stems. These ramify into branches, and these again into twig vessels; all these nadi put together are 727,210,201.

Now, of these the one is the susumna; the rest are divided half and half over the two halves of the body. So we read in the Kathopnishat, 6th valli, 16th mantra:

"A hundred and one nadi are connected with the heart. Of these one passes out into the head. Going out by that one becomes immortal. The others become the cause in sending the life principle out of various other states."

This one that goes to the head, remarks the commentator, is the susumna. The susumna then is that nadi whose nervous substratum or reservoir of force is the spine. Of the remaining principal nadis, the Ida is the reservoir of the life force that works in the left part of the body, having 50 principal nadi. So also has the right part of the body 50 principal nadi. These go on dividing as above. The nadi of the third degree become so minute as to be visible only by a microscope. The ramifications of the susumna all over the body serve during life to carry the prana from the positive to the negative portions of the body, and vice versa. In case of blood these are the modern capillaries.

The Vedantins, of course, take the heart to be the starting point of this ramification. The Yogis, however, proceed from the navel. Thus in The Science of Breath we read: "From the root in the navel proceed 72,000 nadi spreading all over the body. There sleeps the goddess Kundalini like a serpent. From this center (the navel) ten nadi go upwards, ten downwards, and two and two crookedly."

The number 72,000 is the result of their own peculiar reckoning. It matters little which division we adopt if we understand the truth of the case.

Along these nadi run the various forces that form and keep up the physiological man. These channels gather up into various parts of the body as centers of the various manifestations of prana. It is like water falling from a hill, gathering into various lakes, each lake letting out several streams. These centers are:

(1) Hand power centers, (2) Foot power centers, (3) Speech power centers, (4) Excretive power centers, (5) Generative power centers, (6) Digestive and absorbing power centers, (7) Breathing power centers, and (8) the five sense power centers.

Those nadi that proceed to the outlets of the body perform the most important functions of the body, and they are hence said to be the ten principal ones in the whole system. These are:

(1) Ghandari goes to the left eye; (2) Hastijihiva goes to the right eye; (3) Pasta goes to the right ear; (4) Yashawani goes to the left ear; (5) Alamhusha, or alammukha (as it is variously spelled in one ms.) goes to the mouth. This evidently is the alimentary canal; (6) Kuhu goes to the generative organs; (7) Shankini goes to the excretive organs; (8) Ida is the nadi that leads to the left nostril; (9) Pingala is the one that leads to the right nostril. It appears that these names are given to these local nadi for the same reason that the pulmonary manifestation of prana is known by the same name; (10) Susumna has already been explained in its various phases and manifestations.

There are two more outlets of the body that receive their natural development in the female: the breasts. It is quite possible that the nadi Danini, of which no specific mention has been made, might go to one of these. Whatever it may be, the principle of the division and classification is clear, and this is something actually gained.

Centers of moral and intellectual powers also exist in the system. Thus we read in the Vishramopnishat (The following figure will serve to illustrate the translation):

"(1) While the mind rests in the eastern portion (or petal), which is white in color, then it is inclined towards patience, generosity, and reverence.

"(2) While the mind rests in the southeastern portion, which is red in color, then it is inclined towards sleep, torpor and evil inclination.
"(3) While the mind rests in the southern portion, which is black in color, then it is inclined towards anger, melancholy, and bad tendencies.

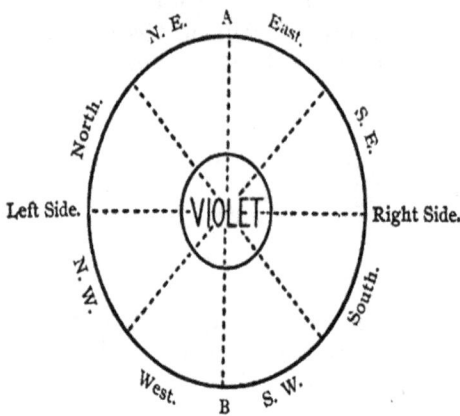

"(4) While the mind rests in the southwestern portion, which is blue in color, then it is inclined towards jealousy and cunning.

"(5) While the mind rests in the western portion, which is brown in color, then it is inclined towards smiles, amorousness, and jocoseness.

"(6) While the mind rests in the northwestern portion, which is indigo in color, then it is inclined towards anxiety, restless dissatisfaction, and apathy.

"(7) While the mind rests in the northern portion, which is yellow in color, then it is inclined towards love and enjoyment and adornment.

"(8) While the mind rests in the northeastern portion, which is white in color, then it is inclined towards pity, forgiveness, reflection, and religion.

"(9) While the mind rests in the sandhi (conjunctions) of these portions, then disease and confusion in body and home, and the mind inclines towards the three humors.

"(10) While the mind rests in the middle portion, which is violet in color, then Consciousness goes beyond the qualities [three qualities of Maya] and it inclines toward Intelligence."

When any of these centers is in action the mind is conscious of the same sort of feelings, and inclines towards them. Mesmeric passes serve only to excite these centers.

These centers are located in the head as well as in the chest, and also in the abdominal region and the loins, etc.

It is these centers, together with the heart itself, that bear the name of padma or kamala (lotus). Some of these are large, some small, some very small. A tantric lotus is the type of a vegetable organism, a root with various branches. These centers are the reservoirs of various powers, and hence the roots of the padma; the nadi ramifying these centers are their various branches.

The nervous plexus of the modern anatomists coincide with these centers. From what has been said above it will appear that the centers are constituted by blood vessels. But the only difference between the nerves and the blood vessels is the difference between the vehicles of the positive and negative prana. The nerves are the positive, and the blood vessels are the negative system of the body. Wherever there are nerves there are corresponding blood vessels. Both of them are indiscriminately called nadi. One set has for its center the lotus of the heart, the other the thousand-petalled lotus of the brain. The system of blood vessels is an exact picture of the nervous system; it is, in fact, only its shadow. Like the heart, the brain has its upper and lower divisions -- the cerebrum and the cerebellum – and its right and left divisions as well. The nerves going to very part of the body and coming back from thence together with those going to the upper and lower portions correspond to the four petals of the heart. This system, too, has as many centers of energy as the former. Both these centers coincide in position. They are, in fact, the same: the nervous plexuses and ganglia of modern anatomy. Thus, in my opinion, the tantric padma are not only the centers of nervous power – the positive northern prana – but necessarily of the negative prana as well.

The translation of the Science of Breath that is now presented to the reader has two sections enumerating the various actions that are to be done during the flow of the positive and negative breath. They show nothing more than what can in some cases be very easily verified, that certain actions are better done by positive energy, and others by negative energy. The taking in of chemicals and their changes are actions, as well as any others. Some of the chemicals are better assimilated by the negative for example, milk and other fatty substances), others by the positive Prana (other food, that which is digested in the stomach). Some of our sensations produce more lasting effects upon the negative, others upon the positive prana.

Prana has now arranged the gross matter in the womb into the nervous and blood vessel systems. The Prana, as has been seen, is made of the five tatwa, and the nadi serve only as lines for tatwic currents to run on. The centers of power noticed above are centers of tatwic power. The tatwic centers in the right part of the body are solar, and those in the left are lunar. Both these solar and lunar centers are of five descriptions. Their kind is determined by what are called the nervous ganglia. The semi-lunar ganglia are the reservoirs of the apas tatwa. Similarly, we have the reservoirs of the other forces. From these central reservoirs the tatwic currents run over the same lines, and do the various actions allotted to them in physiological anatomy.

Everything in the human body that has more less of the cohesive resistance is made up of the prithivi tatwa. But in this the various tatwas work imprinting differing qualities upon the various parts of the body.

The vayu tatwa, among others, performs the functions of giving birth to, and nourishing the skin; the positive gives us the positive, and the negative the negative skin. Each of these has five layers:

(1) Pure vayu, (2) Vayu-agni, (3) Vayu-prithivi, (4) Vayu-apas, (5) Vayu-akasa. These five classes of cells have the following figures:

(1) Pure Vayu ~ This is the complete sphere of the Vayu:

(2) Vayu-Agni ~ The triangle is superposed over the sphere, and the cells have something like the following shape:

(3) Vayu-Prithivi ~ This is the result of the superposition of the quadrangular Prithivi over the spherical Vayu:

(4) Vayu-Apas ~ Something like an ellipse, the semi-moon superposed over the sphere:

5) Vayu-Akasa ~ The sphere flattened by the superposition of the circle and dotted:

A microscopic examination of the skin will show that the cells of the skin have this appearance. Similarly, bone, muscle and fat are given birth to by the prithivi, the agni, and the apas. Akasa appears in various positions. Wherever there is any room for any substance, there is akasa. The blood is a mixture of nutritive substances kept in the fluidic state by the apas tatwa of Prana.

It is thus seen that while Terrestrial Prana is an exact manifestation of the Solar Prana, the human manifestation is an exact manifestation of either. The microcosm is an exact picture of the macrocosm. The four petals of the lotus of the heart branch really into twelve nadi (K, Kh, g, gn, n, K, Kh, j, jh, n, t, the). Similarly the brain has twelve pairs of nerves. These are the twelve signs of the Zodiac, both in their positive and negative phases. In every sign the sun rises 31 times. Therefore we have 31 pairs of nerves. Instead of pairs, we speak in the language of the Tantras of a chakra (disk or circle). Wherever these 31 chakra connect with the 12 pairs (chakras) of nerves in the brain, pass throughout the body, we have running side by side the blood vessels proceeding from the 12 nadis of the heart. The only difference between the spinal and cardiac chakras is that the former lie crosswise, while the latter lie lengthwise in the body. The sympathetic chords consist of lines of tatwic centers: the padma or kamal. These centers lie on all the 31 chakra noticed above. Thus from the two centers of work, the brain and the heart, the signs of the Zodiac in their positive and negative aspects – a system of nadi branch off. The nadi from either center run into one another so much that one set is found always side by side with the other. The 31 chakra are various tatwic centers; one set is positive, and the other is negative. The former owe allegiance to the brain, with which they are connected by the sympathetic chords; the latter owe allegiance to the heart, with which they have various connections. This double system is called Pingala on the right side, and Ida on the left. The ganglia of the apas centers are semi-lunar, those of the taijas, the vayu, the prithivi, and the akasa respectively triangular, spherical, quadrangular, and circular. Those of the composite tatwa have composite figures. Each tatwic center has ganglia of all the tatwa surrounding it.

Prana moves in this system of nadi. As the sun passes into the sign of Aries in the Macrocosm, the Prana passes into the corresponding nadi (nerves) of the brain. From thence it descends every day towards the spine. With the rise of the sun it descends into the first spinal chakra towards the right. It thus passes into the Pingala. It moves along the nerves of the right side, at the same time passing little by little into the blood vessels. Up to noon of every day the strength of this Prana is greater in the nervous chakra than in the venous. At noon they become of equal strength. In the evening (with sunset), the Prana with its entire strength has passed into the blood vessels. From thence it gathers up into the heart, the negative southern center. Then it spreads into the left side blood vessels, gradually passing into the nerves. At midnight the strength is equalized; in the morning (pratasandhia) the prana is just in the spine; from thence it begins to travel along the second chakra. This is the course of the solar current of prana. The moon gives birth to other minor currents. The moon moves 12 odd times more than the sun. Therefore, while the sun passes over one chakra (i.e., during 60 ghari – day and night), the moon passes over 12 odd chakra. Therefore we have 12 odd changes of prana during 24 hours. Suppose the moon too begins in Aries; she begins like the sun in the first chakra, and takes 58 min. 4 sec. in reaching the spine to the heart, and as many minutes from the heart back to the spine.

Both these prana move in their respective course along the tatwic centers. Either of them is present at any one time all over the same class of tatwic centers, in any one part of the body. It manifests itself first in the vayu centers, then in the taijas, thirdly in the prithivi, and fourthly in the apas centers. Akasa comes after each, and immediately precedes the susumna. As the lunar current passes from the spine towards the right, the breath comes out of the right nostril, and as long as the current of Prana remains in the back part of thebody, the tatwa changes from the vayu to the apas. As the current passes into the front part of the right half, the tatwa changes back from the apas to the vayu. As the prana passesinto the heart, the breath is not felt at all in the nose. As it proceeds from the heart to the left, the breath begins to flow out of the left nostril, and as long as it is in the front part of the body, the tatwa change from the vayu to the apas. They change back again a before, until the prana reaches the spine, when we have the akasa of susumna. Such is the even change of prana that we have in the state of perfect health. The impulse that has been given to the localized prana by the sun and moon forces that give active power and existence to its prototype Prana, makes it work in the same way forever and ever. The working of the human free will and other forces change the nature of the local prana, and individualize it in such a way as to render it distinguishable from the universal Terrestrial and Ecliptical prana. With the varying nature of prana, the order of the tatwa and the positive and negative currents may be affected in various degrees.

Disease is the result of this variation. In fact, the flow of breath is the truest indication of the changes of tatwa in the body. The balance of the positive and negative currents of tatwa results in health, and the disturbance of their harmony in disease. The science of the flow of breath is therefore of the highest importance to every man who values his own health and that of his fellow creatures. At the same time, it is the most important, useful and comprehensive, the easiest and the most interesting branch of Yoga. It teaches us how to guide our will so as to effect desired changes in the order and nature of our positive and negative tatwic currents. This it does in the following way. All physical action is prana in a certain state. Without prana there is no action, and every action is the result of the differing harmonies of tatwic currents. Thus, motion in any one part of the body is the result of the activity of the vayu centers in that part of the body. In the same way, whenever there is activity in the prithivi centers, we have a feeling of enjoyment and satisfaction. The causes of the other sensations are similar.

We find that while lying down we change sides when the breath passes out of that nostril. Therefore we conclude that if we lie on any side the breath will flow out the opposite nostril. Therefore, whenever we see that it is desirable to change the negative conditions of our body to the positive, we resort to this expedient. An investigation into the physiological effects of prana on the gross coil, and the counter effects of gross action upon prana, will form the subject of the next essay.

V. Prana (II)

The Pranamaya Kosha (Coil of Life) changes into three general states during day and night: the waking, the dreaming, and the sleeping (jagrata, swapna, susupti). These three changes produce corresponding changes in the manamaya Kosha (the mental coil), and thence arises the consciousness of the changes of life. The mind, in fact, lies behind the prana. The strings (tatwic lines) of the former instrument are finer than those of the latter; that is, in the former we have a greater number of vibrations than in the latter during the same space of time. Their tensions stand to each other, however, in such a relation that with the vibrations of the one, the other of itself begins to vibrate. The changes give to the mind, therefore, a similar appearance, and consciousness of the phenomenon is caused. This, however, some time after. My present object is to describe all those changes of prana, natural or induced, that make up the sum total of our worldly experience, and which, during ages of evolution, have called the mind itself out of the state of latency. These changes, as I have said, divide themselves into three general states: the waking, the dreaming, and the sleeping. Waking is the positive, sleeping the negative state of prana; dreaming is the conjunction of the two (susumna sandhi). As stated in the foregoing essay, the solar current travels in a positive direction during the day, and we are awake. As night approaches the positive current has made itself lord of the body. It gains so much strength that the sensuous and active organs lose sympathy with the external world. Perception and action cease, and the waking state passes off. The excess of the positive current slackens, as it were, the tatwic chords of the different centers of work, and they accordingly cease to answer to the ordinary ethereal changes of external nature. If at this point the strength of the positive current passed beyond ordinary limits, death would ensue, prana would cease to have any connection with the gross body, the ordinary vehicle of the external tatwic changes. But just at the moment the prana passes out of the heart, the negative current sets in, and it begins to counteract the effects of the former. As the prana reaches the spine, the effects of the positive current have entirely passed of, and we awake. If at this moment the strength of the negative current passes the ordinary limit by some cause or other, death would ensue, but just at this moment the positive current sets in with midnight, and begins to counteract the effect of the former. A balance of the positive and negative currents thus keeps body and soul together. With excess in the strength of either current, death makes its appearance. Thus we see that there are two kinds of death: the positive or spinal, and the negative or cardiac. In the former the four higher principles pass out of the body through the head, the brahma-randhra, along the spine; in the latter they pass out of the mouth through the lungs and the trachea. Besides these there are generally speaking about six tatwic deaths. All these deaths chalk out different paths for the higher principle. Of these, however, more hereafter. At this stage, let us investigate the changes of prana more thoroughly.

There are certain manifestations of prana that we find equally at work in all three states. As I have said before, some writers have divided these manifestations into five heads.

They have different centers of work in different parts of the body, from whence they assert their dominion over every part of the physical coil. Thus:

Positive: (1) Prana, right lung; Negative: Prana, left lung. Prana is that manifestation of the life coil which draws atmospheric air from without into the system.

Positive: (2) Apana, the apparatus that passes off feces, long intestine, etc.; Negative: Apana, the urinary apparatus. Apana is the manifestation that throws, from the inside, out of the system, things that are not wanted there.

Positive: (3) Samana, stomach; Negative: Samana, duodenum. Samana is that manifestation which draws in and carries the juice of food to every part of the body.

Positive: (4) Vyana, all over the body, appearing in varying states with different organs (on the right side); Negative: Vyana, all over the body (on the left side). Vyana is that manifestation which inclines the currents of life back to the centers – the heart and the brain. It is, therefore, this manifestation that causes death, local or general.

Positive: (5) Udana, at the spinal and cardiac centers (right side), and the region of the throat; Negative: Udana, the spinal and cardiac centers (left side).

If Prana recedes from any part of the body (for some reason or other), that part loses its power of action. This is local death. It is in this way that we become deaf, dumb, blind, etc. It is in this way that our digestive powers suffer, and so on. General death is similar in its operations. With the excess of the strength of either of the two currents, the prana remains in the susumna, and does not pass out. The acquired power of work of the body then beings to pass off. The farther from the centers (the heart and the brain), the sooner they die. It is thus that the pulse first ceases to be felt in the extremities, and then nearer and nearer the heart, until we find it nowhere.

Again, it is this upward impulse that, under favorable conditions, causes growth, lightness, and agility.

Besides the organs of the body already mentioned or indicated, the manifestation of vyana serves to keep in form the five organs of sense, and the five organs of action. The organs of the gross body and the powers of prana that manifest themselves in work have both the same names. Thus we have:

Active Organs & Powers: (1) Vak, the coal organs and the power of speech; (2) Pani, the hands and the manual power; (3) Pada, the feet and the walking power; (4) Payu, anus; (5) Upastha, the generative organs and the powers that draw these together.

Sensuous Organs & Powers: (1) Chaksus, eye and ocular power; (2) Twak, skin and tangiferous power; (3) Srotra, ear and sonoriferous power; (4) Rasama, tongue and gustatory power; (5) Cobrana, nose and odoriferous power.

The real fact is that the different powers are the corresponding organs of the principle of life. It will now be instructive to trace the tatwic changes and influences of these various manifestations of life.

Prana: During health prana works all over the system in one class of tatwic centers at one time. We thus see that both during the course of the positive and negative current we have five tatwic changes. The color of prana during the reign of the positive and negative current is pure white; during that of the positive, reddish white. The former is calmer and smoother than the latter.

The tatwic changes give to each of these five new phases of color. Thus: Positive ~ reddish white/ Negative ~ pure white:
(1) The vayu tatwa, blue; (2) The agni tatwa, red; (3) The prithivi, yellow; (4) The apas,

It is evident that there is a difference between the positive and negative tatwic phases of color. There are thus ten general phases of color.

The positive current (reddish white) is hotter than the negative (the pure white). Therefore it may be generally said that the positive current is hot, and the negative cool. Each of these then undergoes five tatwic changes of temperature. The agni is the hottest, the yellow next to it; the vayu becomes cool, and the apas is the coolest. The akasa has a state that neither cools nor heats. This state is the most dangerous of all, and if prolonged it causes death, disease and debility. It is evident that, if the cooling tatwa does not set in to counteract the accumulated effect of the latter in due time, the functions of life will be impaired. The just color and the just temperature at which these functions work in their vigor will be disturbed, and disease, death and debility are nothing more than this disturbance in various degrees. The case is similar if the heating tatwa does not set in in due time after the cooling one.

It will be easy to understand that these changes of tatwic colors and temperatures are not abrupt. The one passes of easily and smoothly into the other, and the tatwic mixtures produce innumerable colors – as many, in fact, as the solar prana has been shown to possess. Each of these colors tend to keep the body healthy if it remains in action just as long as it ought, but no sooner does the duration change than disease results. There is a possibility, therefore, of as many and more diseases as there are colors in the sun.

If any one color is prolonged, there must be some one or more that have given the period of their duration to it; similarly, if one color takes less time than it ought to, there must be some one or more that take its place. This suggests two methods of the treatment of diseases. But before speaking of these, it will be necessary to investigate as fully as possible the causes that lengthen and shorten the ideal periods of the tatwas.

To return at present to Prana: This pulmonary manifestation of the principle of life is the most important of all, because its workings furnish us with a most faithful measure of the tatwic state of the body. It is on this account that the name prana has been given by pre- eminence to this manifestation.

Now, as the prana works in the pulmonary taijas centers (i.e., the centers of the luminiferous ether), the lungs are thrown into a triangular form of expansion, atmospheric air runs in, and the process of inspiration is complete. With every truti, a backwards impulse is given to the currents of prana. The lungs are thrown into their stationary state with this returning current, and the excess air is expelled. The air that is thus thrown out of the lungs bears a triangular form. To some extent, the water vapor that this air contains furnishes us with a method of testing this truth by experiment. If we take a smooth, shining looking glass, put it under the nose, and breath steadily upon its cool surface, the water vapor of the air will be condensed, and it will be seen that this bears a particular figure. In the case of pure agni, this figure will be a triangle. Let another person look steadily at the looking glass because the impression passes off rather quickly.

With the course of the other tatwas the lungs are thrown into their respective shapes, and the looking glass gives us the same figures. Thus, in apas we have the semi-moon, in vayu the sphere, and in prithivi the quadrangle. With the composition of these tatwas we may have other figures: oblongs, squares, spheroids, and so on.

It may also be mentioned that the luminiferous ether carries the materials drawn from the atmospheric air to the centers of the luminiferous ether, and thence to every part of the body. The other ethers also carry these materials to their respective centers. It is not necessary to trace the working of the other manifestations one by one. It may, however, be said that although all the five tatwas work in all the five manifestations, each of these manifestations is sacred to one of these tatwas. Thus in prana the vayu tatwa prevails, in samana the agni, in apana the prithivi, in vyana the apas, in udana the akasa. I may remind the reader that the general color of prana is white, and this will show how the apas tatwa prevails in Vyana. The darkness of akasa is the darkness of death, etc., caused by the manifestation of udana.

During life these ten changes are always taking place at the intervals of about 26 minutes each. In waking, in sleep, or in dream, these changes never cease. It is only in the two susumnas or the akasa that these changes become potential for a moment, because it is from these that these tatwic manifestations show themselves on the plane of the body. If this moment is prolonged, the forces of prana remain potential, and in death the prana is thus in the potential state. When those causes that tended to lengthen the period of i, and thus cause death, are removed, this individual prana passes out of the potential into the actual, positive, or negative state as the case may be. It will energize matter, and will develop it into the shape towards which its accumulated potentialities tend.

Something may now be said about the work of the sensuous and active organs.

It may be generally said that all work is tatwic motion. This work is capable of being carried on during the waking state, and not in sleep or dream. These ten organs have ten general colors, generally thus:

Sensuous Organs: (1) Eye, agni, red; (2) Ear, akasa, dark; (3) Nose, prithivi, yellow; (4) Tongue (taste), apas, white; (5) Skin, vayu, blue;

Active Organs: (1) Hand, vayu, blue; (2) Foot, i, yellow; (3) Tongue (speech), apas, white; (4) Anus, akasa, dark; (5) Genitals, i, red.

Although these are the generally prevalent tatwas in these various centers, all the other tatwas exist in a subordinate position. Thus in the eye we have a reddish yellow, reddish white, reddish dark, reddish blue, and similarly in the other organs. This division into five of each of these colors is only general; in reality there is an almost innumerable variation of colors in each of these.

With every act of every one of these ten organs, the organ specially and the whole body generally assumes a different color, the color of that particular tatwic motion which constitutes that act.

All these changes of Prana constitute the sum total of our worldly experience. Furnished with this apparatus, prana begins its human pilgrimage, in company with a mind, which is evolved only to the extent of connecting the "I am" of the ahankara or vijnana, the fourth principle from below, with these manifestations of prana. Time imprints upon it all the innumerable colors of the universe. The visual, the tangible, the gustatory, the auditory, and the olfactory appearances in all their variety gather into prana just as our daily experience carries many messages at one and the same time. In the same way do the appearances of the active organs, and the five remaining general functions of the body, gather up in this prana to manifest themselves in due time.

A few illustrations will render all this clear:

Sexual Relations ~

The generative agni tatwa of the male is positive, and that of the female is negative. The former is hotter, harsher, and more restless than the latter; the latter is cooler, smoother, and calmer than the former. These two currents tend to run into each other, and a feeling of satisfaction is the result if the two currents are allowed to take their course; if not, a feeling of uneasiness is the result. The genesis of these feelings will be my subject under the head of the manomaya kosha (mental principle). Here I shall only speak of the coloration of prana by the action or inaction of this organ. The positive agni tends to run into the negative, and vice versa. If it is not allowed to do so, the repeated impulses of this tatwa turn upon themselves, the center gains strength, and every day the whole prana is colored deeper and deeper red. The centers of the agni tatwa all over the body become stronger in their action, while all the others contract a general tinge of the red. The eyes and the stomach become stronger. This, however, is the case only within certain limits and under certain circumstances. If the agni gains too much strength, all the other centers of the remaining tatwas become vitiated in their action by an over-coloration of agni, and disease and debility result. If, however, man indulges in this luxury more often than he should, and in more than one place, the male prana gets colored by the female agni, and vice versa. This tends to weaken all the centers of this tatwa, and gives a feminine color to the whole prana. The stomach becomes cooled down, the eyes grow weak, and virile manly power departs. If, however, more than one individual female agni takes possession of the male prana, and vice versa, the general antagonistic tatwa becomes deeper and stronger. The whole prana is vitiated to a greater extent, greater debility is the result, and spermatorrhea, impotence, and other such antagonistic colors take possession of the prana. Besides, the separate individualities of the male or female agni that has taken possession of any one prana will tend to repel each other.

Walking ~

Suppose now that a man is given to walking. The prithivi tatwa of the feet gains strength, and the yellow color pervades the whole prana. The centers of the prithivi all over the body begin to work more briskly; agni receives a mild and wholesome addition to its power, the whole system tends towards healthy equilibrium, neither too hot, nor too cold, and a general feeling of satisfaction accompanied with vigor, playfulness, and a relish of enjoyment is the result.

Speech ~

Let me take one more illustration from the operation of Vak (speech), and I shall be done with the organs of action. The power (Sakti) of speech (Vak, saraswati) is one of the most important goddesses of the Hindu pantheon. The apas tatwa is the chief ingredient of prana that goes towards the formation of this organ. Therefore the color of the goddess is said to be white. The vocal chord with the larynx in front form the vina (musical instrument) of the goddess.

In the above figure of the vocal apparatus, AB is the thyroid, a broad cartilage forming the projection of the throat, and much more prominent in men than in women. Below this is the annular cartilage C, the crecoid. Behind this, or we may say on this, are stretched the chord a and b.

Atmospheric air passing over these chords in the act of breathing sets these chords in vibration, and sound is the result. Ordinarily these chords are too loose to give any sound. The apas tatwa, the milk-white goddess of speech, performs the all-important function of making these chords tense. As the semi-lunar current of the apas tatwa passes along the muscles of these chords, they are as it were shriveled up and curves are formed in the chords; they become tighter.

The depth of these curves depends upon the strength of the apas current. The deeper these curves, the tenser are the chords. The thyroid serves to vary the intensity of the voice thus produced. The thyroid serves to vary the intensity of the voice thus produced. This will do here, and it is enough to show that the real motive power in the production of voice is the apas tatwa or Prana. As will be easily understood, there are certain ethereal conditions of the external world that excite the centers of the apas tatwa; the current passes along the vocal chords, they are made tense, and sound is produced. But the excitement of these centers also comes from the soul through the mind. The use of this sound in the course of evolution as the vehicle of thought is the marriage of Brahma (the Vijana mayakosha, the soul) with Saraswati, the power of speech as located in man.

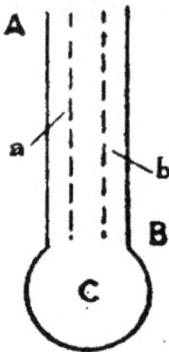

The apas tatwa of the vocal apparatus, although it is the chief motive power in the production of sound, is modified according to the circumstance by the composition of the other tatwas in various degrees. As far as human ken reaches, about 49 of these variations have been recorded under the name of swara. First, there are seven general notes. These may be positive and negative (tivra and komala), and then each of these may have three subdivisions. These notes are then composed into eight raga, and each raga has several ragini. The simple ragini may then be compounded into others, and each ragini may have a good many arrangements of notes. The variations of sound thus become almost innumerable. All these variations are caused by the varying tensions of the vocal chords, the Vina of Saraswati, and the tensions vary by the varying strength of the apas current, caused by the superposition of the other tatwas.

Each variation of sound has a color of its own that affects the whole prana in its own way; the tatwic effect of all these sounds is noted in books of music. Various diseases may be cured, and good or bad tendencies imprinted on the prana by the power of sound. Saraswati is an all-powerful goddess, and controls our prana for good or evil as the case may be. If a song or note is colored by the agni tatwa, the sound colors the prana red, and similarly the vayu, the apas, the akasa, and the prithivi, blue, white, dark, and yellow. The red colored song causes heat; it may cause anger, sleep, digestion, and redness of color.

The akasa colored song causes fear, forgetfulness, etc. Songs may similarly give our prana the color of love, enmity, adoration, morality, or immorality, as the case may be.

Let us turn to another key. If the words we utter bear the color of the agni tatwa – anger, love, lust – our prana is colored red, and this redness turns upon ourselves. It may burn up our substance, and we may look lean and lank and have 10,000 other diseases. Terrible retribution of angry words! If our words are full of divine love and adoration, kindness and morality, words that give pleasure and satisfaction to whoever hears them – the colors of the prithivi and the apas – we become loving and beloved, adoring and adored, kind and moral, pleasing and pleased, satisfying and ever satisfied. The discipline of speech itself – the satya of Patanjali – is thus one of the highest practices of Yoga.

Sensuous impressions color the prana in a similar way. If we are given to too much of sight- seeing, to the hearing of pleasant sounds, to the smelling of dainty smells, etc., the colors of these tatwas will be overly strengthened, and will gain a mastery over our prana. If we are too fond of seeing beautiful women, hearing the music of their voices, heaven help us, for the least and most general effect will be that our pranas will receive the feminine coloration. If it were only for the love of women, man should avoid this over-indulgence, for feminine qualities in men do not obtain favor in the eyes of women.

These illustrations are sufficient to explain how the tatwic colors of external nature gather up in prana. It may be necessary to say that no new colors enter into the formation of prana. All the colors of the universe are present there already, just as they are in the sun, the prototype of prana. The coloration I have spoken of is only the strengthening of this particular color to an extent that throws the others in shade. It is this disturbance of balance that in the first place causes the variety of human prana, and in the second those innumerable diseases to which flesh is heir.

From this point it is evident that every action of man gives his prana a separate color, and the color affects the gross body in turn. But when, at what time, does the particular tatwic color affect the body? Ordinarily it is under similar tatwic conditions of the external universe. This means that if the agni tatwa has gained strength in any prana at any one particular division of time, the strength will show itself when that particular division of time recurs again. Before attempting a solution of this problem, it is necessary to understand the following truths:

The sun is the chief life-giver of every organism in the system. The moment that a new organism has come into existence, the sun changes his capacity in relation to that organism. He now becomes the sustainer of positive life in that organism. Along with this the moon begins to influence the organism in her own way. She becomes the sustainer of negative life. The planets each establish their own currents in the organism. For the sake of simplicity, I have as yet spoken only of the sun and moon, the respective lords of the positive and negative currents of the right and left halves of the body, of the brain and the heart, of the nerves and the blood vessels. These are the two chief sources of life, but it must be remembered that the planets exercise a modifying influence over these currents. The real tatwic condition of any moment is determined by all the seven planets, just like the sun and the moon. Each planet, after determining the general tatwic condition of the moment, goes to introduce changes in the organism born at that moment. These changes correspond with the manifestation of that color of prana that rose at that time. Thus, suppose the red color has entered prana when the moon is in the second degree of the sign of Libra. If there is no disturbing influence of any other luminary, the red color will manifest itself whenever the moon is in the same position; in the other case, when the disturbing influence is removed. It may show itself in a month, or it may be postponed for ages. It is very difficult to determine the time when an act will have its effect. It depends a good deal upon the strength of the impression. The strength of the impression may be divided into ten degrees, although some writers have gone further.

(1) Momentary: This degree of strength has its effect then and there;

(2) 30 degrees strength: In this case the effect will show itself when each planet is in the same sign as at the time of the impression;
(3) 15 degrees strength: Hora; (4) 10 degrees strength: Dreskana; (5) 200 degrees strength: Navaansha; (6) 150 degrees strength: Dwadasansa; (7) 60 or 1 degree strength: Trinsansa; (8) 1" strength: Kala; (9) 1'" strength: Vipala; (10) 1'"" strength: Truti.

Suppose in any prana, on account of any action, the agni tatwa obtains the strongest possible prevalence consistent with the preservation of the body, the tatwa will begin to have its effect then and there until it has exhausted itself to a certain extent. It will then become latent and show itself when at any time the same planets sit in the same mansions. Examples will illustrate better. Suppose the following advancement of the planets at any moment denotes the tatwic condition when any given color has entered the prana:

It is at this time, we suppose, that the act above referred to is committed. The present effect will pass off with the two hours' lunar current that may be passing at that time. Then it will become latent, and remain so till the time when these planets are in the same position again. As has been seen, these positions might be nine or more in number.

As soon as the exact time passes of when a color has obtained predominance in prana, the effect thereof on the gross body becomes latent. It shows itself again in a general way when the stars sit in the same mansions. Some of the strength is worn off at this time, and the force becomes latent to show itself in greater minuteness when at any time the half- mansions coincide, and so on with the remaining parts noticed above. There may be any number of times when there is only an approach to coincidence, and then the effect will tend to show itself, though at that time it will remain only a tendency.

These observation, although necessarily very meager, tend to show that the impression produced upon prana by any act, however insignificant, really takes ages to pass off, when the stars coincide in position to a degree with that when the act was committed. Therefore, a knowledge of astronomy is highly essential in occult Vedic religion. The following observation may, however, render the above a little more intelligible.

As often remarked, the prana mayokosha is an exact picture of the Terrestrial Prana. The periodical currents of the finer forces of

The 3rd of April, Tuesday ~

Planet	Sign	Degree	Minute	Second
Sun	11	22	52	55
Moon	8	16	5	9
Mercury	10	25	42	27
Venus	11	26	35	17
Mars	5	28	1	40
Jupiter	7	15	41	53
Saturn	3	9	33	30

nature that are in the earth pass according to the same laws in the principle of life; just like the Zodiac, the prana mayakosha is subdivided into
mansions, etc. The northern and southern inclinations of the axis give us
a heart and a brain. Each of these has 12 ramifications branching off from
it; these are the 12 signs of the Zodiac. The daily rotation than gives us the
31 chakras spoken of previously. There is the positive semi-mansion and
the negative semi-mansion. Then we have the one-third, the one-ninth,
the one-twelfth, and so on to a degree, or the divisions and subdivisions
thereof. Each chakra, both diurnal and annual, is in fact a circle of 360
degrees, just like the great circles of the heavenly spheres. Through the
chakra a course of seven descriptions of life- currents is established:

(1) Solar, (2) lunar, (3) Mars, agni, (4) Mercury, prithivi, (5) Jupiter,
vayu, (6) Venus, apas, (7) Saturn, akasa.

It is quite possible that along the same chakra there may be passing all
or any one or more of these differing currents at one and the same time.
The reader is reminded of the telegraph currents of modern electricity.
It is evident that the real state of prana is determined by the position of
these localized currents. Now if any one or more of these tatwic currents
is strengthened by any act of ours, under any position of the currents, it is
only when we have to a degree the same position of the currents that
the tatwic current will makes it appearance at full strength. There may
also be appearances of slight power at various times, but the full strength
will never be exhausted until we have the same position of these currents
to the minutest division of a degree. This takes ages upon ages, and it is
quite impossible that the effect should pass off in the present life. Hence
rises the necessity of a second life upon this earth.

The accumulated tatwic effects of a life's work give each life a general
tinge of its own. This tinge wears off gradually as the component colors
pass off or weaken in strength, one by one. When each of the component
colors is one by one sufficiently worn off, the general color of a life passes
off. The gross body that was given birth to by this particular color ceases
to respond to the now generally different colored prana. The prana does
not pass out of the susumna. Death is the result.

Death ~

As already said, the two ordinary forms of death are the positive
through the brain, and the negative through the heart. This is death
through the susumna. In this all the tatwas are potential. Death may also
take place through the other nadis. In this case there must always be the
prevalence of one or more tatwas.

The prana goes towards different regions after death, according to the paths through which it passes out of the body. Thus:

(1) The negative susumna takes it to the moon; (2) the positive susumna takes it to the sun; (3) the agni of the other nadi takes it to the hill known as Raurava (fire); (4) the apas of the other nadi takes it to the hill known as Ambarisha, and so on, the akasa, the vayu, and the prithivi take it to Andhatanusra, Kalasutra, and Maha kala (See Yoga Sutra, pada 111, Aphorism 26, commentary).

The negative path is the most general one that the prana takes. This path takes it to the moon (the chandraloka) because the moon is the lord of the negative system, and the negative currents, and the negative susumna the heart, which therefore is a continuation of the lunar prana. The prana that has the general negative color cannot move but along this path, and it is transferred naturally to the reservoirs, the centers of the negative prana. Those men in whom the two hours' lunar current is passing more or less regularly take this path.

The prana that has lost the intensity of its terrestrial color energizes lunar matter according to its own strength, and thus establishes for itself there a sort of passive life. Here the mind is in a state of dream. The tatwic impressions of gathered up forces pass before it in the same way as they pass before it in our earthly dreams. The only difference is that in that state there is not the superimposed force of indigestion to render the tatwic impressions so strong and sudden as to be terrible. That dreamy state is characterized by extreme calmness. Whatever our mind has in it of the interesting experiences of this world, whatever we have thought, heard, seen or enjoyed, the sense of satisfaction and enjoyment, the bliss and playfulness of the apas and the prithivi tatwa, the languid sense of love of the agni, the agreeable forgetfulness of the akasa, all make their appearance one after the other in perfect calm. The painful impressions make no appearance, because the painful arises when any impression forces itself upon the mind that is out of harmony with its surroundings. In this state the mind lives in Chandraloka, as will be better understood when I come to speak of the tatwic causes of dreams.

Ages roll on in this state, when the mind has, according to the same general laws that obtain for prana, worn out the impressions of a former life. The intense tatwic colors that the ceaseless activity of prana had called into existence now fade away, until at last the mind comes upon a chronic level with the prana. Both of them have now lost the tinge of a former life. It may be said of prana that it has a new appearance, and of the mind that it has a new consciousness. When they are both in this state, both very weak, the accumulated tatwic effects of prana begin to show themselves with the return of the stars to the same positions. These draw us back from the lunar to the terrestrial prana. At this stage, the mind has no individuality worth taking account of, so that it is drawn by prana to wherever its affinities carry it. It comes and joins with those solar rays that bear a similar color, with all those mighty potentialities that show themselves in the future man remaining quite latent. It passes with the rays of the sun according to the ordinary laws of vegetation into grain that bears similar colors. Each grain has a separate individuality, which accounts for its separate individuality from others of its brothers, and in many there may be human potentialities giving it an individuality of its own. The grain or grains produce the virile semen, which assumes the shape of human beings in the wombs of women. This is rebirth.

Similarly do human individualities come back from the five states that are known as hells. These are the states of posthumous existence fixed for those men who enjoy to an excessive and violent degree the various impressions of each of the tatwas. As the tatwic intensity, which disturbs the balance and therefore causes pain, wears off in time, the individual prana passes off to the lunar sphere, and thence undergoes the same states that have been described above.

Along the positive path through the brahmarandhra pass those prana that pass beyond the general effects of Time, and therefore do not return to the earth under ordinary laws. It is Time that brings back prana from the moon, when he is even the most general, and the least strong tatwic condition comes into play with the return of identical astral positions; but the sun being the keeper of Time himself, and the strongest factor in the determination of his tatwic condition, it would be impossible for solar Time to affect solar prana. Therefore, only that prana travels towards the sun in which there is almost no preponderance of any tatwic color.

This is the state of the prana of Yogin alone. By the constant practice of the eight branches of Yoga, the prana is purified of any very strongly personifying colors, and since it is evident that on such a prana Time can have no effect, under ordinary circumstances, they pass off to the sun. These prana have no distinct personifying colors; all of them that go to the sun have almost the same general tinge. But their minds are different. They can be distinguished from each other according to the particular branch of science that they have cultivated, or according to the particular and varying methods of mental improvement that they have followed on earth. In this state the mind is not dependent, as in the moon, upon the impressions of prana. Constant practice of Yoga has rendered it an independent worker, depending only upon the soul, and molding the prana to its own shapes, and giving it its own colors. This is a kind of Moksha.

Although the sun is the most potent lord of life, and the tatwic condition of prana now has no effect upon the prana that has passed to the sun, the planetary currents still have some slight effect upon it, and there are times when this effect is very strong, so that the earthly conditions in which they have previously lived are called back again to their minds. A desire to do the same sort of good they did the world in their previous life takes possession of them, and impelled by this desire they sometimes come back to earth. Snakaracharya has noticed in his commentary of the Brahmasutra that Apantaramah, a Vedic rishi, thus appeared on earth as Krishna-dwaipayana, about the end of the Dwapara and the beginning of the Kaliyuga.

VI. Prana (III)

As it is desirable that as much as possible should be known about Prana, I give below some quotations on the subject from the Prasnopnishat. They will give additional interest to the subject, and present it in a more comprehensive and far more attractive garb.

Six things are to be known about Prana, says the Upanishad:

"He who knows the birth (1), the coming in (2), the places of manifestation (3), the rule (4), the macrocosmic appearance (5), and the microcosmic appearance of Prana becomes immortal by that knowledge."

Practical knowledge of the laws of life, i.e., to live up to them, must naturally end in the passing of the soul out of the shadowy side of life into the original light of the Sun. This means immortality, that is, passing beyond the power of terrestrial death.

But to go on with what the Upanishad has to say about the six things to be known about Prana:

The Birth of Prana ~

The Prana is born from the Atma; it is caused in the atma, like the shadow in the body. The human body, or any other organism, becomes the cause of throwing a shade in the ocean of prana, as it comes between the sun and the portion of space on the other side of the organism. Similarly, the prana is thrown as a shade in the macrocosmic soul (Iswara) because the macrocosmic mind (manu) intervenes. Briefly the prana is the shade of Manu caused by the light of the Logos, the macrocosmic center. The suns are given birth to in this shade, by the impression of the macrocosmic mental ideas into this shade. These suns, the centers of Prana, become in their turn the positive starting point of further development. The manus throwing their shade by the intervention of the suns, give birth in those shades to planets, etc. The suns throwing their shades by the intervention of planets, give birth to moons. Then these different centers begin to act upon the planets, and the sun descends on the planets in the shape of various organisms, man included.

The Macrocosmic Appearance ~

This prana is found in the macrocosm as the ocean of life with the sun for its center. It assumes two phases of existence: (1) the prana, the solar, positive life-matter, and (2) the rayi, the lunar, negative life-matter. The former is the northern phase and the eastern; the latter is the southern phase and the western. In every Moment of Terrestrial life, we have thus the northern and southern centers of prana, the centers from which the southern and northern phases of life-matter take their start at any moment. The eastern and western halves are there too.

At every moment of time – i.e., in every truti – there are millions of truti – perfect organisms – in space. This might require some explanation. The units of time and space are the same: a truti.

Take any one truti of time. It is well known that every moment of time the tatwic rays of prana go in every direction from every point to every other point. Hence it is clear enough that every truti of space is a perfect picture of the whole apparatus of prana, with all its centers and sides, and positive and negative relations. To express a good deal in a few words, every truti of space is a perfect organism. In the ocean of Prana that surrounds the sun there are innumerable such truti.

While essentially the same, it is easy to understand that the following items will make a difference in the general color, appearance, and forms of these trutis: (1) distance from the solar center; (2) inclination from the solar axis.

Take the earth for illustration. That zone of solar life, taking into consideration both the distance and the inclination in which the earth moves, gives birth to earth-life. This zone of earth-life is known as the ecliptic. Now every truti of space in this ecliptic is a separate individual organism. As the earth moves in her annual course, i.e., as the truti of time changes, these permanent truti of space change the phases of their life. But their permanency is never impaired. They retain their individuality all the same.

All the planetary influences reach these trutis always, wherever the planets may be in their journey. The changing distance and inclination is, of course, always causing a change of life-phase.

This truti of space, from its permanent position in the ecliptic, while maintaining its connection with all the planets, at the same time sends its tatwic rays to every other quarter of space. They also come to the earth.

It is a condition of earth life that the positive and negative currents, the prana and the rayi, be equally balanced. Therefore, when the two phases of life matter are equally strong in this ecliptical truti, the tatwic rays that come from it to the earth energize gross matter there. The moment that the balance is disturbed by the tatwic influence of the planets, or by some other cause, terrestrial death ensues. This simply means that the tatwic rays of the truti that fall on earth cease to energize gross matter, although they do fall there all the same, and although the truti is there all the same in its permanent ecliptical abode. In this posthumous state, the human truti will energize gross matter in that quarter of space whose laws of relative, negative and positive predominance coincide with that state. Thus, when the negative life matter, the rayi, becomes overly strong, the energization of the truti is transferred from the earth to the moon. Similarly it may pass to other spheres. When the terrestrial balance is restored again, when this posthumous life has been lived, the energization is transferred to the earth again.

Such is the macrocosmic appearance of Prana, with the pictures of all the organisms of the earth.

The Coming In Of Prana ~

How does this prana maya kosha – this truti of the macrocosm – come into this body? Briefly, "By actions at whose root lies the mind", says the Upanishad. It was explained previously how every action changes the nature of the prana maya kosha, and it will be explained in the essay on the "Cosmic Picture Gallery" how these changes are represented in the cosmical counterpart of our life-principle. It is evident that by these actions change is produced in the general relative nature of the prana and the rayi, which has been spoken of previously. It is hardly necessary to say that the mind – the human free will – lies at the root of those actions that disturb the tatwic balance of the life-principle. Hence, "The prana comes into this body by actions, at whose root lies the mind."

The Places of Manifestation ~

"As the paramount Power appoints its servants, telling, 'Rule such and such villages', so does the Prana. It puts its different manifestations in different places. The apana (this discharges faces and urine) is in the Payu (anus) and the upastha. The manifestations known as sight and hearing (Chakahus and Srotra) are in the eye and ear. The prana remains itself, going out of mouth and nose. Between (the places of prana and apana, about the navel) lives the Samana. It is this that carries equally (all over the body) the food (and drink) that is thrown in the fire. Hence are those seven lights (by means of prana, light of knowledge is thrown over color, form, sound, etc.)

"In the heart is of course this atma (the pranamaya kosha) and in it, of course, the other coils. Here there are a hundred and one nadi. Of these there are a hundred in each. In each of these branch nadis there are 72,000 other nadi. In these moves the vyana.

"By one (the Susumna) going upward, the udana carries to good worlds by means of goodness, and to bad ones by means of evil; by both to the world of men.

"The sun is, of course, the macrocosmic prana; he rises, and thereby helps the eyesight. The Power that is in the earth keeps up the power of apana. The akasa (the ethereal matter) that is between heaven and earth, helps the samana.

"The ethereal life-matter (independent of its being between heaven and earth) which fills macrocosmic space, is vyana.

"The taijas – the luminfierous ether – is udana; hence he whose natural fire is cooled down approaches death.

"Then the man goes toward the second birth; the organs and senses go into the mind; the mind of the man comes to the Prana (its manifestations now ceasing). The prana is combined with the taijas; going with the soul, it carries her to the spheres that are in view."

The different manifestations of Prana in the body, and the places where they manifest themselves have been dwelt upon. But other statements of interest appear in this extract. It is said that this atma, this prana maya kosha, with the other coils of course, is located in the heart. The heart, as has been seen, represents the negative side of life, the rayi.

When the positive prana impresses itself upon the rayi – the heart and the nadis that flow from it– the forms of life and the actions of man come into existence. It is therefore, properly speaking, the reflection in the heart that works in the world, i.e., is the proper lord of the sensuous and active organs of life. If this being of the heart learns not to live here, the sensuous and active organs both lose their life; the connection with the world ceases. The being of the brain that has no immediate connection with the world, except through the heart, now remains in unrestrained purity. This means to say that the soul goes to the suryaloka (the Sun).

The next point of interest is the description of the functions of the External Prana, which lie at the root of, and help the working of the individualized prana. It is said that the Sun is the Prana. This is evident enough, and has been mentioned man times before this. Here it is meant to say that the most important function of life, inspiration and expiration, the function of which, according to the Science of Breath, is the One Law of existence in the Universe on all the planes of life, is brought into existence and kept in activity by the sun in himself. It is the solar breath that constitutes his existence, and this reflected in man producing matter gives birth to human breath.

The Sun then appears in another phase. He rises, and as he does, he supports the eyes in their natural action.

Similarly, the power that is in the earth sustains the apana manifestation of prana. It is the power that draws everything towards the earth, says the commentator. In modern language, it is gravity.

Something more might be said here about the udana manifestation of prana. As everybody knows, there is a phase of microcosmic prana that carries everything, names, forms, sight, sounds, and all other sensations, from one place to another. This is otherwise known as the universal agni, or the Tejas of the text. The localized manifestation of Prana is called udana, that which carries the life-principle from one place to another. The particular destination is determined by past actions, and this universal agni carries the prana, with the soul, to different worlds.

VII. Prana (IV)

This Prana is then a mighty being, and if its localized manifestations were to work in unison, and with temperance, doing their own duty, but not usurping the time and place of others, there would be but little evil in the world.

But each of these manifestations asserts its sole power over the bewildered human soul. Each of these claims the whole life of man to be its own proper domain:

"The akasa, the vayu, the agni, the prithivi, the apas, speech, sight and hearing – all of them say clearly that they are the sole monarchs of the human body."

The principal prana, he whose manifestations all these are, tells them:

"Be not forgetful; it is I who sustain the human body, dividing myself into five."

If the five manifestations of Prana with all their minor subdivisions revolt against him, if each begin to assert its own lordship and cease to work for the general benefit of the lord paramount, the real life, misery makes its sad appearance to harass the poor human soul. "But the manifestation of prana, blinded by ignorance," would not "put forth" in the admonitions of their lord. "He leaves the body, and as he leaves, all the other minor pranas leave it too; they stay there as he stays." Then their eyes are opened. "As the bees follow the queen bee in every posture, so does prana; these, speech, the mind, the eye, the ear, follow him with devotion, and thus praise him."

"He is the agni, the cause of heat; he is the sun (the giver of light); he is the cloud, he is the Indra, he is the Vayu, he is the prithivi, he is the rayi, and the deva, the sat, and the asat, and he is the immortal.

[Rayi and asat are the negative, deva and sat the positive phases of life-matter.]

"Like the spokes in the nave of a wheel, everything is sustained in prana: the hymns of the Rik, the Yajur, and the Sama Veda, the sacrifice, the Kshatriya, and the Brahmin, etc.

"Thou art the Progenitor; thou movest in the womb; thou art born in the shape of the father or the mother; to thee, O Prana, that puts up in the body with thy manifestations, these creatures offer presents.

"Thou art the carrier of offerings to the deva, thou art the carrier of oblations to the fathers; thou art the action and the power of the senses and other manifestations of life.

"Thou art, O Prana, in power the great lord, the Rudra [the destroyer] and the Preserver; thou movest in the sky as the sun, thou art the preserver of the light of heaven.

"When thou rainest, these creatures are full of joy because they hope to have plenty of food.

"Thou art Prana, pure by nature; thou art the consumer of all oblations, as the Ekarshi fire [of the Atharva; thou art the preserver of all existence; we are to thee the offerers of food; thou art our father as the Recorder [or, the Life-giver of the Recorder].

"Make healthy that appearance of thine which is located in the speech, the ear, the eye, and that which is stretched towards the mind; do not fly away.

"Whatever exists in the three heavens, all of it is in the power of prana. Protect us like a mother her offspring; give us wealth and intellect."

With this I conclude my description of Prana, the second principle of the Universe, and the human body. The epithets bestowed upon this mighty being in the above extract will be easy of understanding in the light of all that has gone before. It is now time to trace the working of the universal Tatwic Law of Breath on the next higher pane of life, the mind (manomayakosha).

VIII. *The Mind (I)*

Introduction~

No theory of the life of the Universe is at once so simple and so grand as the theory of breath (Swara). It is the one universal motion, which makes its appearance in maya by virtue of the unseen substratum of the Cosmos, the parabrahma of the Vedantins. The most appropriate expression for Swara in English is the "current of life". The Indian Science of Breath investigates and formulates the laws, or rather the one Universal Law, according to which this current of life, this motive power of Universal Intelligence, running (as Emerson so beautifully puts it) along the wire of thought, governs evolution and involution and all the phenomena of human life, physiological, mental and spiritual. In the whole length and breadth of this universe there is no phenomenon, great or small, that does not find its most natural, most intelligible, most apposite explanation in the theory of the five modes of manifestation of this universal motion: the five elementary tatwas. In the foregoing essays I have tried to explain generally how every physiological phenomenon was governed by the five tatwas. The object of the present essay is to briefly run over the various phenomena relating to the third higher body of man – the manomaya kosha, the mind – and note how symmetrically and universally the tatwas bring about the formation and work of this principle.

Knowledge ~

It is what is in general language called knowledge that distinguishes the mind from physiological life (prana), but it will be seen on a little consideration that different degrees of knowledge might very well be taken as the distinguishing characteristics of the five states of matter, which in man we call the five principles. For what is knowledge but a kind of tatwic motion of breath, elevated into self-consciousness by the presence, in a greater or lesser degree, of the element of ahankara (egoism)? His is no doubt the view taken of knowledge by the Vedantic philosopher when he speaks of intelligence as being the motive power, the first cause of the universe. The word swara is only a synonym of intelligence, the one manifestation of the One descending into prakriti.

"I see something" means, according to our view of knowledge, that my manomaya kosha has been put into visual vibration. "I hear" means that my mind is in a state of auditory vibration. "I feel" means that my mind is in a state of tangible vibration. And so on with the other senses. "I love" means that my mind is in a state of amatory vibration (a form of attraction).

The first state, that of the anandamaya, is the state of the highest knowledge. There is then but one center, the substratum for the whole infinity of parabrahma, and the ethereal vibrations of his breath are one throughout the whole expanse of infinity. There is but one intelligence, but one knowledge. The whole universe with all its potentialities and actualities is a part of that knowledge. This is the highest state of bliss. There is no consciousness of self here, for the I has only a relative existence, and there must be a Thou or a He before there can be an I.

The ego takes form when, in the second plane of existence, more than one minor center comes into existence. It is for this reason that the name ahankara has been given to this state of matter. The ethereal impulses of those centers are confined to their own particular domain in space, and they differ in each center. They can, however, affect each other in just the same way as the individualized ethereal impulses of one man are affected by those of others. The tatwic motion of one center of Brahma is carried along the same universal lines to the other. Two differing motions are thus found in one center. The stronger impulse is called the I, the weaker the Thou or the He as the case may be.

Then comes manas. Viraj is the center, and manu the atmosphere of this state. These centers are beyond the ken of ordinary humanity, but they work under laws similar to those ruling the rest of the cosmos. The suns move the virats in the same way as the planets move around the sun.

The Functions of the Mind ~

The composition of the manu is similar to that of prana: it is composed of a still finer grade of the five tatwas, and this increased fineness endows the tatwas with different functions.

The five functions of prana have been given. The following are the five functions of manas, as given by Patanjali and accepted by Vyasa:

(1) Means of knowledge (Pramana), (2) False knowledge (Viparyaya), (3) Complex imagination (Vikalpa), (4) Sleep (Nidra), (5) Memory (Smrite).

All the manifestation of the mind fall under one or another of these five heads. Thus, Pramana includes:

(1) Perception (pratyaksha), (2) Inference (anumana), (3) Authority (Agama).

Viparyana includes:

(1) Ignorance (avidya, tamas), (2) Egoism (asinita, moha), (3) Retention (raja, mahamoka), (4) Repulsion (tamisra, dwesha), (5) Tenacity of life (abhinwesha, andhatamisra).

The remaining three have no definite subdivisions. Now I shall show that all the modifications of thought are forms of tatwic motion on the mental plane.

Pramana (Means of Knowledge) ~

The word pramana (means of knowledge) is derived from two roots, the predicative ma, and the derivative root ana, with the prefix pra. The original idea of the root ma is "to go", "to move", and hence "to measure". The Prefix pra gives the root idea of fullness, connected as it is with the root pri, to fill. That which moves exactly up or down to the same height with any other thing is the pramana of that thing. In becoming the pramana of any other thing, the first thing assumes certain qualities that it did not have before. This is always brought about by a change of state caused by a certain kind of motion, for it is always motion that causes change of state. In fact, this is also the exact meaning of the word pramana, as applied to a particular manifestation of the mind.

Pramana is a particular tatwic motion of the mental body; its effect is to put the mental body into a state similar to that of something else. The mind can undergo as many changes as the external tatwas are capable of imprinting upon it, and these changes have been classified into three general heads by Patanjali.

Pratyaksha (Perception) ~

This is that change of state which the operations of the five sensuous organs produce in the mind. The word is a compound of "I", each, and "aksha", sensuous power, organ of sense. Hence is that sympathetic tatwic vibration that an organ of sense in contact with its object produces in the mind. These changes can be classified under five heads, according to the number of the senses.
The eye gives birth to the taijas vibrations, the tongue, the skin, the

ear, and the nose respectively to the apas, the vayu, the akasa and the prithivi vibrations. The pure agni causes the perception of red, the taijas-prithivi of yellow, the taijas-apas of white, the taijas-vayu of blue, and so on. Other colors are produced in the mind by mixed vibrations in a thousand varying degrees. The apas gives softness, the vayu roughness, the agni harshness. We see through the eyes not only color, but also form. It will be remembered that a particular form has been assigned to every tatwic vibration, and all the forms of gross matter answer to correspond-ing tatwic vibrations. Thus, form can be perceived through every sense. The eyes can see form, the tongue can taste it, the skin can touch it, and so on. This may probably appear to be a novel assertion, but it must be remembered that virtue is not an act. The ear would hear form, if the more general use of the eye and skin for this purpose had not almost stifled it into inaction.

The pure apas vibrations cause an astringent taste, the apas-prithivi a sweet, the apas-agni hot, the apas-vayu acid, and so on. Innumerable other vibrations of taste are caused by intermediate vibrations in various degrees.

The case is similar with the vocal and other changes of vibration. It is clear that our perceptive knowledge is nothing more than a veritable tatwic motion of the mental body, caused by the sympathetic commu-nications of the vibrations of prana, just as a stringed instrument of a certain tension begins to vibrate spontaneously when vibration is set up in another similar instrument.

Anumana (Inference) ~

The word anumana has the same roots as the word pramana. The only difference is in the prefix. We have here anu, "after", instead of pra. Inference (anumana) is therefore after- motion. When the mind is capable of sustaining two vibrations at one and the same time, then if any one of these vibrations is set up and perceived, the second vibration must also manifest itself. Thus, suppose a man pinches me. The complex vibrations that make up the perception of the action of man pinching me are pro-duced in my mind. I recognize the phenomena. Almost simultaneously with these vibrations another set of vibrations is produced in me. I call this pain. Now here are two kinds of tatwic motion, one coming after the other. If at any other time I feel similar pain, the image of the man pinch-ing will be recalled to my consciousness. This after-motion is "inference". Induction and deduction are both modifications of this after-motion. The sun always appears to rise in a certain direction. The concept of that direction becomes forever associated in my mind with the rising of the sun. Whenever I think of the phenomenon of sunrise, the concept of that direction presents itself. Therefore I say that, as a rule, the sun rises in that direction. Inference is therefore nothing more than a tatwic motion coming after another related one.

Agama (Authority) ~

The third modification of what is called the means of knowledge (pramana) is authority (agama). What is this? I read in my geography, or hear from the lips of my teacher that Britain is surrounded by the ocean. Now what has connected these words in my mind with the picture of Britain, the ocean, and their mutual relations? Certainly it is not perception, and therefore not inference, which must by nature work through sensuous knowledge. What then? There must be some third modification.

The fact that words possess the power to raise a certain picture in our minds is one of very deep interest. Every Indian philosopher recognizes it as a third modification of the mind, but it receives no recognition at the hands of modern European philosophy.

There is, however, little doubt that the color corresponding to this mental modification differs from that corresponding to either perception or inference. The color belonging the perceptive modifications of the mind is always single in nature. A certain phase of the taijas vibration must always prevail in the visual modification, and similarly the vibrations of other tatwas correspond to our different sensuous modifications. Each manifestation has its own distinctive color. The red will appear as well in the visual as in the auditory or any other vibration, but the red of the visual will be bright and pure; that of the organ of smell will be tinged with yellow; that of the organ of touch with blue, and the soniferous ether will be rather dark. There is, therefore, not the least likelihood that the vocal vibration will coincide with the pure perceptive vibration. The coal vibrations are double in their nature, and they can only (if at all) coincide with the inferential vibrations; and here, too, they can only coincide with the auditory vibrations. A little consideration will, however, show that there is some difference between the vocal and inferential vibrations. In inference, a certain modification of sound in our mind is followed by a certain visual picture, and both these vibrations retain an equally important position in our mind. We place two precepts together, compare them, and then say that one follows the other. In the verbal modification there is no comparison, no simultaneous consciousness, no placing together of the two precepts. The one causes the other, but we are not at all conscious of the fact. In inference the simultaneous presence for some time of both the cause and the effect brings about a change in the color of the effect. The difference is less great in the vocal as compared with the inferential vibration. Axiomatic knowledge is not inferential in the present, tough it has no doubt been so in the past; in the present it has become native to the mind.

Viparyaya (False Knowledge) ~

This is the second mental modification. This word also is derived from a root meaning motion : i or ay. "to go", "to move". The prefix pari is connected with the root pra, and gives the same radical meaning as pramana. The word Paryaya has the same radical meaning as pramana. The word Viparyaya therefore means "a motion removed from the motion that coincides with the object". The vibrations of pramana coincide in nature with the vibrations of viparyaya. Certain acquired conditions of the mind imprint on the precepts a new color of their own, and thus distinguish them from the precepts of pramana. There are five modifications of this manifestation.

Avidya (Ignorance) ~

This is the general field for the manifestation of all the modifications of false knowledge. The word comes from the root vid, "to know", the prefix a, and the suffix ya. The original meaning of the vidya is, therefore, "the state of a thing as it is", or expressed in terms of the mental plane in one word, "knowledge". As long as in the face of a human being I see a face and nothing else, my mental vibration is said to be vidya. But as soon as I see a moon or something else not a face, when it is a face I am looking at, my mental vibration is no longer said to be vidya, but avidya. Avidya (ignorance) is therefore not a negative conception; it is just as positive as vidya itself. It is a great mistake to suppose that words having the privative prefixes always imply abstractions and never realities. This, however, is by the bye. The state of avidya is that state in which the mental vibration is disturbed by that of akasa, and some other tatwas, which thus result in the production of false appearances. The general appearance of avidya is akasa, darkness, and this is why tamas is a synonym of this word.

This general prevalence of darkness is caused by some defect in individual minds, because, as we find from daily experience, a given object does not excite the same set of vibrations in all minds. What, then is the mental defect? It is to be found in the nature of the stored-up potential energy of the mind. This storing-up of potential energy is a problem of the deepest importance in philosophy, and the doctrine of transmigration of souls finds its most intelligible explanation in this. The law might be enunciated as follows:

The Law of Vasana ~

If anything be set in any particular kind of tatwic motion, internal or external, it acquires for a second time the capability of easily being set in motion, and of consequently resisting a different sort of motion. If the thing is subjected to the same motion for some time, the motion becomes a necessary attribute of the thing. The superposed motion becomes, so to speak, "second nature".

Thus, if a man accustoms his body to a particular form of exercise, certain muscles in his body are very easily set into motion. Any other form of exercise that requires the use of other muscles will be found fatiguing on account of the resistance set up by muscular habits. The case is similar with the mind. If I have a deep-rooted conviction, as some do to this day, that the earth is flat and the sun moves around it, it may require ages to dislodge it. A thousand examples might be cited of such phenomena. It is, however, only necessary in this place to state that the capacity of turning easily to one mental state and offering resistance to another one is what I mean by this stored-up energy. It is variously called vasana or Sansakara in Sanskrit.

The word vasana comes from the root vas, "to dwell". It means the dwelling or fixing of some form of vibratory motion in the mind. It is by vasana that certain truths become native to the mind, and not only certain so-called truths, but all the so-called natural tendencies, moral, physical, spiritual, become in this way native to the mind. The only difference in different vasana is their respective stability. The vasana that are imprinted upon the mind as the result of the ordinary evolutionary course of nature never change.

The products of independent human actions are of two kinds. If actions result in tendencies that check the evolutionary progressive tide of nature, the effect of the action exhausts itself in time by the repellant force of the undercurrent of evolution. If, however, the two coincide in direction, increased strength is the result. The latter sort of actions we call virtuous, the former vicious.

It is this vasana, this temporary dominion of the opposite current, that causes false knowledge. Suppose the positive generative current has in any man the strength a, if too it is presented a negative female current of the same degree of strength a, the two will try to unite. An attraction that we term sexual love will then be set up. If these two currents are not allowed to unite, they increase in strength and react on the body itself to its injury; if allowed to unite, they exhaust themselves. This exhaustion causes a relief to the mind, the progressive evolutionary current asserts itself with greater force, and thus a feeling of satisfaction is the result. This tatwic disturbance of the mind will, as long as it has sufficient strength, give its own color to all perceptions and concepts. They will not appear in their true light, but as causes of satisfaction. Thus they say that true lovers see all things rose-colored. The appearance of a face we love to see causes a partial running of currents into one another, and a certain amount of satisfaction is the result. We forge that we are seeing a face: we are only conscious of some cause resulting in a state of satisfaction. That cause of satisfaction we call by different names. Sometimes we call it a flower, at others we call it a moon. Sometimes we feel that the current of life is flowing from those dear eyes, at others we recognize nectar itself in that dear embrace. Such are the manifestations of avidya. As Patanjali says, avidya consists in the perception of the eternal, the pure, the pleasing, and the spiritual instead of or rather in the non-eternal, the impure, the painful, and the non-spiritual. Such is the genesis of avidya, which, as has been remarked, is a substantial rality, and not a mere negative conception.

This mental phenomenon causes the four remaining ones.

Asmita (Egoism) ~

Egoism (Asmita) is the conviction that real life (purusha swara) is one with the various mental and physiological modifications, that the higher self is one with the lower one, that the sum of our percepts and concepts is the real ego, and that there is nothing beyond. In the present cycle of evolution and in the previous ones, the mind has been chiefly occupied with these percepts and concepts. The real power of life is never seen making any separate appearance, hence the feeling that the ego must be the same with the mental phenomena. It is plain that avidya, as defined above, lies at the root of this manifestation.

Raga (Desire to Retain) ~

The misleading feeling of satisfaction above mentioned under avidya is the cause of this condition. When any object repeatedly produces in our mind this feeling of satisfaction, our mind engenders the habit of falling again and again into the same state of tatwic vibration. The feeling of satisfaction and the picture of the object that seemed to cause that satisfaction tend to appear together, and this is a hankering after the object, a desire not to let it escape us – that is to say, Raga.

Pleasure ~

Here may investigate more thoroughly the nature of this feeling of satisfaction and its opposite: pleasure and pain. The Sanskrit words for these two mental states are respectively sukha and dukkha. Both come from the root khan, "to dig"; the prefixes su and dus make the difference. The former prefix conveys the idea of "ease" and it derives this idea from the unrestrained easy flow of breath. The radical idea of sukha is, therefore, unrestrained digging – digging where the soil offers but little resistance. Transferred to the mind, that act becomes sukha, which makes an easy impression upon it. The act must, in the nature of its vibrations, coincide with the then prevailing conditions of the mental vibrations. Before any percepts or concepts had taken root in the mind, there was no desire, no pleasure. The genesis of desire and what is called pleasure – that is, the sense of satisfaction caused by the impressions produced by external objects – begins with certain percepts and concepts taking root in the mind. This taking root really is only an overclouding of the original set of impressions arising out of evolutionary mental progress. When contact with the external object momentarily removes that cloud from the clear horizon of the mind, the soul is conscious of a feeling of satisfaction that avidya connects with the external object. This, as shown above, gives birth to desire.

Pain & Dwesha ~

The genesis of pain and the desire to repel (dwesha) is similar. The radical idea of dukkha (pain) is the act of digging where a good deal of resistance is experienced. Transferred to the mind, it signifies an act that encounters resistance from the mind. The mind does not easily give place to these vibrations; it tries to repel them with all its might. There arises a feeling of privation. It is as if something of its nature was being taken away, and an alien phenomenon introduced. The consciousness of privation, or want, is pain, and the repulsive power that these alien vibrations excite in the mind is known by the name of dwesha (desire to repel). The word dwesha comes from the root dwesh, which is a compound of du and ish. Ish itself appears to be a compound root, i and s. The final s is connected to the root su, "to breath", "to be in one's natural state". The root i means "to go", and the root ish, therefore, means to go toward one's natural state. Transferred to the mind, the word becomes a synonym of raga. The word du in dwesh performs the same function as dus in dukkh. Hence dwesh comes to mean "a hankering after repulsion". Anger, jealousy, hatred, etc., are all modifications of this, as love, affection and friendship are those of raga. By what has been said above, it is easy to follow up the genesis of the principle of "tenacity of life". I must now try to assign these actions to their prevailing tatwas.

The general color of avidya is, as already said, that of akasa, darkness. Otherwise, the agni tatwa prevails in anger. If this is accompanied by vayu, there will be a good deal of motion in the body, prithivi will make it stubborn, and apas easily manageable. Akasa will give a tinge of fear.

The same tatwa prevails in love. Prithivi makes it abiding, vayu changeable, agni fretting, apas lukewarm, and akasa blind.

Akasa prevails in fear; it tends to produce a hollow in the veins themselves. In prithivi the timid man is rooted to the spot, with vayu he runs away, with apas he succumbs to flattery, and agni tends to make one vengeful.

Vikalpa ~

Vikalpa is that knowledge which the words imply or signify, but for which there is no reality on the physical plane. The sounds of nature connected with its sight have given us names for precepts. With the additions or subtractions of the percepts we have also had additions and subtractions of the sounds connected therewith. The sounds constitute our words.

In vikalpa two or more precepts are added together in such a way as to give birth to a concept having no corresponding reality on the physical plane. This is a necessary result of the universal law of visana. When the mind is habituated to a perception of more phenomena than one, all of them have a tendency to appear again; and whenever two or more such phenomena coincide in time, we have in our mind a picture of a third something. That something may or may not exist in the physical plane. If it does not, the phenomenon is vikalpa. If it does, however, we call it Samadhi.

This also is a phenomenon of the manomaya kosha mind. Indian philosophers speak of three states in this connection: waking, dream, and sleep.

Waking ~

This is the ordinary state when the principle of life works in connection with the mind. The mind then receives impressions of the external objects through the action of the senses.

The other faculties of the mind are purely mental, and they may work in the waking as in the dreaming state. The only difference is that in dreams the mind does not undergo the perceptive changes. How is this? These changes of state are always passive, and the soul has no choice in being subjected to them. They come and go as a necessary result of the working of swara in all its five modifications. As has been explained in the articles on Prana, the different sensuous organs cease to respond to external tatwic changes when the positive current gains more than ordinary strength in the body. The positive force appears to us in the shape of heat, the negative in the shape of cold. Therefore I may speak of these forces as heat and cold.

Dreams ~

The Upanishad says that in dreamless sleep the soul sleeps in the blood vessels (nadi), the pericardium (puritat), the hollow of the heart. Has the system of blood vessels, the negative center of Prana, anything to do with dreams also? The state of dream, according to the Indian sage, is an intermediate one between waking and sleeping, and it is but reasonable to suppose that there must be something in this system that accounts for both these phenomena. What is that something? It is variously spoken of as the pitta, the agni, and the sun. It is needless to say that these words are meant to denote one and the same thing. It is the effect produced on the body by the solar breath in general, and the agni tatwa in particular. The word pitta might mislead many, and therefore it is necessary to state that the word does not necessarily always mean lull. There is one pitta that Sanskrit physiology locates specifically in the heart. This is called the sadhaka pitta. It is nothing more or less than cardiac temperature, and it is with this that we have to do in sleep or dream.

According to the Indian philosopher, it is the cardiac temperature that causes the three states in varying degrees. This and nothing more is the meaning of the Vedic text that the soul sleeps in the pericardium, etc. All the functions of life are carried on properly as long as we have a perfect balance of the positive and negative currents, heat and cold. The mean of the solar and lunar temperatures is the temperature at which the prana keeps up its connection with the gross body. The mean is struck after an exposure of a whole day and night. Within this period the temperature is subjected to two general variations. The one is the extreme of the positive; the other the extreme of the negative. When the positive reaches its daily extreme the sensuous organs pass out of time with the external tatwas.

It is a matter of daily experience that the sensuous organs respond to external tatwic vibrations within certain limits. If the limit is exceeded either way, the organs become insensible to these vibrations. There is, therefore, a certain degree of temperature at which the sensuous organs can ordinarily work; when this limit is exceed either way, the organs become incapable of receiving any impression from without. During day the positive life current gathers strength in the heart. The ordinary working temperature is naturally exceeded by this gathering up of the forces, and the senses sleep. They receive no impression from without. This is sufficient to produce the dreaming state. As yet the chords of the gross body (sthula sharira) alone have slackened, and the soul sees the mind no longer affected by external impressions. The mind is, however, habituated to various precepts and concepts, and by the mere force of habit passes into various states. The breath, as it modifies into the five tatwic states, becomes the cause of the varying impressions coming up. As already said, the soul has no part in calling up these visions of its own free will. It is by the working of a necessary law of life that the mind undergoes the various changes of the waking and the sleeping states. The soul does nothing in conjuring up the phantasms of a dream, otherwise it would be impossible to explain horrible dreams. hideous appearances that, with one terrible shock, seem to send our very blood back to our heart? No soul would ever act thus if it could help it.

The fact is that the impressions of a dream change with the tatwas. As one tatwa easily glides into the other, one thought gives place to another. The akasa causes fear, shame, desire, and anger; the vayu takes us to different places; the taijas shows us gold and silver, and the prithivi may bring us enjoyment, smiles, dalliance, and so on. And then we might have composite tatwic vibrations. We might see men and women, dances and battles, councils and popular gatherings; we might walk in gardens, smell the choicest flowers, see the most beautiful spots; we might shake hands with our friends, we might deliver speeches, we might travel into different lands. All these impressions are caused by the tatwic state of the mental coil, brought about either by (1) physical derangement, (2) ordinary tatwic changes, (3) or some other coming natural change of state.

As there are three different causes, there are three different kinds of dreams. The first cause is physical derangement. When the natural currents of prana are disturbed so that disease results, or are about to be so disturbed, the mind in the ordinary way undergoes these tatwic changes. The sympathetic chords of the minds are excited, and we dream of all the disagreeable accompaniments of whatever disease may be within our physical atmosphere in store for us. Such dreams are akin in their nature to the ravings of delirium; there is only a difference in strength and violence. When ill, we may in a similar way dream of health and its surroundings.

The second kind of dream is caused by ordinary tatwic changes. When the past, the present, and the future tatwic condition of our surroundings is uniform in its nature, when there is no change, and when no change is in store for us, the stream of dreams is most calm and equable in its easy flow. As the atmospheric and the healthful physiological tatwas glide smoothly one into the other, so do the impressions of our minds in this class of dreams. Ordinarily we cannot even remember these dreams, for in them there is nothing of special excitement to keep them in our memory.

The third kind of change is similar to the first; there is only a difference in the nature of the effects. These we call the effects of disease or health, as the case may be; here we might group the results under the general name of prosperity or calamity.

The process of this sort of mental excitement is, however, the same in both. The currents of life, pregnant with all sorts of good and evil, are sufficient in strength while yet potential and only tending towards the actual, to set the sympathetic chords of the mind in vibration. The purer the mind, and the freer from dust of the world, the more sensitive it is to the slightest and the remotes tendency of prana towards some change.

Consequently we become conscious of coming events in dreams. This explains the nature of prophetic dreams. To weigh the force of these dreams, however, to find out exactly what each dream means, is a most difficult task, and under ordinary circumstances quite impossible. We may make 10,000 mistakes at ever step, and we need nothing less than a perfect Yogi for the right understanding of even our own dreams, to say nothing of those of others. Let us explain and illustrate the difficulties that surround us in the right understanding of our dreams. A man in the same quarter of the city in which I live, but unknown to me, is about to die. The tatwic currents of his body, pregnant with death, disturb the atmospheric tatwas, and through their instrumentality are spread in various degrees all over the world. They reach me, too, and excite the sympathetic chords of my mind while I am sleeping. There being no special room in my mind for that man, my impression will be only general. A human being, fair or ugly, male or female, lamented or not, and having other similar qualities, will come into the mid on his deathbed. But what man? The power of complex imagination, unless strongly kept in check by the hardest exercise of yoga, will have its play, and it is almost certain that a man who has previously been connected in my mind with all these tatwic qualities will make his appearance in my consciousness. It is evident that I shall be on the wrong track. That someone is dead or dying, we may be sure, but who or where is impossible for ordinary men to discover. And not only does the manifestation of vikalpa put us on the wrong track, but all the manifestations of the mind do that. The state of samadhi, which is nothing more than putting one's self into a state of the most perfect amenability to tatwic surroundings, is therefore impossible unless all the other manifestations are held in perfect check. Patanjali says, "Yoga is keeping in check the manifestations of the mind."

Sleep ~

The dreamy state is maintained as long as and when the cardiac temperature is not strong enough to affect the mental coil. But with increasing positive strength, that too must be affected. The manas and the prana are made of the same materials and are subject to the same laws. The more subtle these materials are, however, the stronger must be the forces that produce similar changes. All the coils are tuned together, and changes in the one affect the other. The vibrations per second of the first one are, however, larger in number than those of the lower one, and this causes its subtlety. The higher are always affected through the immediately lower principles. Thus the external tatwas will affect prana immediately, but the mind can only be affected through the prana and not directly. The cardiac temperature is only an indication of the degree of heat in prana. When sufficient strength is gathered up there, the prana affects the mental coil. That too now passes out of tune with the soul. The mental vibration can only work at a certain temperature; beyond that it must go to rest. In this state we have no more dreams. The only manifestation of the mind is that of rest. This is the state of dreamless sleep.

I pass on now to the fifth and last mental manifestation.

Smrite (Retention, Memory) ~

As Professor Max Muller has remarked, the original idea at the root smri (from which smrite) is "to make soft, to melt". The process of making soft or melting consists in the melting thing assuming a consistency nearer and nearer to the tatwic consistency of the melting force. All change of state is equivalent to the assumption on the part of the thing changing, of the state of tatwa that causes the change. Hence the secondary idea of the root, "to love". Love is that state of mind in which it melts into the state of the object of love. This change is analogous to the chemical change that gives us a photograph on a sensitive plate. As in this phenomenon the materials on the sensitive plate are melted into the state of the reflected light, so the sensitive plate of the mind melts into the state of its percepts. The impression upon the mind is deeper, the greater the force of the imprinting rays and the greater the sympathy between the mind and the object perceived. This sympathy is created by stored up potential energy, and the perceptive rays themselves act with greater force when the mind is in a sympathetic state.

Every percept takes root in the mind, as explained above. It is nothing more than a change of the tatwic state of the mind, and what is left behind is only a capacity for sooner falling into the same state again. The mind falls back into the same state when it is under the influence of the same tatwic surroundings. The presence of the same thing calls back the same mental state.

The tatwic surroundings may be of two descriptions, astral and local. The astral influence is the effect upon the individual prana of the condition of the terrestrial prana at that time. If this effect appears as the agni tatwa, those of our concepts that have a prominent connection with this tatwa will make their appearance in the mind. Some of these are a hankering after wealth, a desire for progeny, etc. If we have the vayu tatwa, a desire to travel may take possession of our minds and so on. A minute tatwic analysis of all of our concepts is of the greatest interest; suffice it to say here that the tatwic condition of prana often calls up into the mind objects that have made the objects of perception in similar previous conditions. It is this power that underlies dreams of one class. In the waking state too this phase of memory often acts as reminiscence.

Local surrounding are constituted by those object which the mind has been accustomed to perceive together with the immediate object of memory. This is the power of association. Both these phenomena constitute memory proper (smrite). Here the object comes first into the mind, and afterwards the act and the surroundings of perception. Another very important kind of memory is what is called buddhi, literary memory. This is the power by which we call to mind what we have learned of scientific facts. The process of storing up these facts in the mind is the same, but the coming back into consciousness differs in this, that here the act first comes into the mind and then the object. All the five tatwas and the foregoing mental phenomena may cause the phenomenon of memory.

Literary memory has a good deal to do with yoga, i.e., the exercise of free will to direct the energies of the mind into desirable channels. While those impressions that take root in the mind on account of natural surroundings make the mind the unwilling slave of the external world, buddhi may lead it to bliss and freedom. But will these tatwic surroundings always bring related phenomena into consciousness? No! This depends upon their correlative strength. It is well known that when the vibrations per second of akasa (sound) pass beyond a certain limit either way, they do not affect the tympanum. It is, for example, only a certain number of vibrations per second of the taijas tatwa that affects the eye, and so on with the other senses. The case with the mind is similar. It is only when mental and external tatwic tensions are equal that the mind begins to vibrate as it comes into contact with the external world. Just as the varying states of the external organs make us more or less sensitive to ordinary sensation, so different men might not hear the same sounds, might not see the same sights, the mental tatwas might not be affected by percepts of the same strength, or might be affected in different degrees by percepts of the same strength. The question is, how is the variation of this mental tatwic strength produced? By exercise, and the absence of exercise. If we accustom the mind, just as we do the body, to any particular precept or concept, the mind easily turns to those percepts and concepts. If, however, we give up the exercise, the mind becomes stiff and ceases by degrees to respond to these percepts and concepts. This is the phenomenon of forgetting. Let a student whose literary exercises is just opening the buds of his mind, whose mind is just gaining strength enough to see into the causes and effects of things, give up his exercise. His mind will begin to lose that nice perception. The stiffer the mind becomes the less will the casual relation affect him, and the less he will know of it, until at last he loses all his power.

Ceaseless influence and activity of one sort being impossible in the ordinary course of time, every impression tends to pass away as soon as it is made. Its degree of stability depends upon the duration of the exercise. But although activity of one sort is impracticable, activity of some sort is always present in the mind. With every action the color of the mind changes, and one color may take so deep a root in the mind as to remain there for ages upon ages, to say nothing of minutes, hours, days and years. Just as time takes ages to demolish the impressions of the physical plane, just as marks of incision upon the skin may not pass away even in two decades, so also it takes ages to demolish the impressions of the mind. Hundreds and thousands of years may this be spent in devachan in order to wear away those antagonistic impressions that the mind has contracted in earthly life. By antagonistic impressions, I mean those impressions that are not compatible with the state of moksha, and have about them a tinge of earthly life.

With every moment the mind changes its color, whether the impression be adding or subtracting. These changes are temporary. But there is at the same time a permanent change going on in the color of the mind. With every little act of our worldly experience, the evolutionary tide of progress is gaining strength and passing into variety. The color is constantly changing. But the same general color is maintained under ordinary circumstances, during one earthly life. Under extraordinary circumstances we might have men having two memories. Under such circumstances as in the case of approaching death, the accumulated forces of a whole life combine into a different color. The tension, so to speak, becomes different from what it was before. Nothing can put the mind into the same state again. This general color of the mind differing from that of other minds, and yet retaining its general character for a whole life, gives us the consciousness of personal identity. In every act that has been done, or that is, or might be done, the soul sees the same general color, and hence the feeling of personal identity. In death the general color changes, and although we have the same mind, we have a different consciousness. Hence no continuance of the feeling of personal identity is possible through death.

Such is a brief account of the manomaya kosha, the mental coil in the ordinary state. The influence of the higher principle (the vijnana maya kosha) through the exercise of yoga induces in the mind a number of other manifestations. Psychic manifestations show themselves in the mind and the prana, in the same way as mental manifestations are seen influencing and regulating the prana.

IX. The Mind (II)

As has been seen, the universe has five planes of existence (which may also be divided into seven). The forms of the earth, which are little pictures of the universe, also have the same five planes. In some of these organisms the higher planes of existence are absolutely latent. In man, in the present age, the Vijnana maya kosha and the lower principles make their appearance.

We have had an insight into the nature of the macrocosmic prana, and we have seen that almost every point in this ocean of life represents a separate individual organism.

The case is similar with the macrocosmic mind. Every truti of that center takes in the whole of the macrocosmic mind in the same way. From every point the tatwic rays of the mental ocean go to every point, and thus every point is a little picture of the universal mind. This is the individual mind.

The Univesal mind is the original of all the centers of Prana, in the same way as the solar prana is the original of the species of earth-life. Individual mind, too, is similarly the original of all the individual manifestations of the prana maya kosha. Similarly the soul, and the individual spirit on the highest plane, is the perfect picture of all that comes below.

With the four higher planes of life there are four different states of consciousness, the waking, the dreaming, the sleeping, and the Tureya.

With these remarks the following extract from the Prasnopnishat will be intelligible and instructive.

"Now Sauryayana Gargya asked him, 'Sir, in this body, what sleeps, and what remains awakened? Which of these luminous beings sees dreams? Who has this rest? In whom do all these [manifestations] rest in the potential unmanifested state?'

"He answered him, 'O Gargya, as the rays of the setting sun are all collected in the luminous shell, and then go out again, as he rises again and again, so all that is collected in the luminous shell of mind beyond. For this reason then, the man does not hear, does not see, does not smell, does not taste, does not touch, does not take, does not cohabit, does not excrete, does not go on. They say that he sleeps. The fires of prana alone remain awakened in his body. The apana is the Garhapatya fire; the Vyana is the right hand fire. The prana is the ahavanurya fire, which is made by the Garhapatya. That which carries equally everywhere the oblations of food and air, is the samana. The mind (manas) is the sacrificer (vajmana). The Udana is the fruit of the sacrifice. He carries the sacrificer every day to Brahma. Here this luminous being [the mind] enjoys great things in dreams. Whatever was seen, he sees again as if it were real; whatever was experienced in different countries, in different directions, he experiences the same again and again – the seen and the unseen, the heard or the unheard, thought or not thought upon. He sees all, appearing as the self of all manifestations.

"'When he is overpowered by the taijas, then this luminous being sees no dreams in this state; then there appears in the body this rest [the dreamless sleep].

"'In this state, my dear pupil, all [that is enumerated below] stays in the ulterior atma, like birds that resort to a tree for habitation – the prithivi composite and the prithivi non- composite; the apas composite and the apas non-composite; the taijas composite and the taijas non-composite; the vayu composite and the vayu non-composite; the akasa composite and the akasa non-composite; the sight and the visible, the hearing and the audible, the smell and the smellable, the taste and the tasteable, the touch and the tangible, the speech and the utterable, the hands and whatever might be grasped, the generative organ and the excrements, the feet and that which may be gone over, the faculty and the object of doubt, the faculty and the object of egoism, the faculty and the object of memory, the light and that which might be enlightened, the prana and that which keeps it together.

"'The soul is the Vijnana atma, the seer, the toucher, the hearer, the smeller, the taster, the doubter, the ascertainer, the agent. This soul [the Vijnana atma] stays in the ulterior, unchangeable atma [the ananda].

"'So there are four atma – the life, the mind, the soul, the spirit. The ultimate force that lies at the root macrocosmic Power of all the manifestation of soul, mind, and the life the principle, is the spirit.'"

By composite is meant that tatwa which has come into existence after the division into five, noticed in the first essay. The non-composite means a tatwa before the division into five.

The principal interest of this quotation lies in presenting in authoritative fashion the views that have already been propounded. The next essay explains one of the most important functions of the macrocosmic Power and Mind, that of recording the human actions, and touches upon some other rather important truths.

X. *The Cosmic Picture Gallery*

We are directed by our Guru in the philosophy of tatwas to look into vacant space toward the sky, when the sky is perfectly clear, and fix your attention there with the utmost possible strength.

We are told that after sufficient practice we shall see there a variety of pictures – the most beautiful landscapes, the most gorgeous palaces of the world, and men, women and children in all the varying aspects of life. How is such a thing possible? What do we learn by this practical lesson in the science of attention?

I think I have described with sufficient explicitness in the essays, the ocean of prana with the sun for its center, and have given a hint sufficiently suggestive of the nature of the macrocosmic mental and psychic atmospheres. It is of the essential nature of these atmospheres that every point therein forms a center of action and reaction for the whole ocean. From what has already been said, it will be plain that each of these atmospheres has a limit of its own. The terrestrial atmosphere extends only to a few miles, and the external boundary line of this sphere must, it will be readily understood, give it the appearance of an orange, just like that of the earth. The case is the same with the solar prana, and the higher atmospheres. To begin with the terrestrial Prana, which has the measured limits of our atmosphere. Every little atom of our earth, and the most perfect organisms, as well as the most imperfect, makes a center of action and reaction for the tatwic currents of terrestrial Prana. The prana has the capability of being thrown into the shape of every organism or, to use a different language, the rays of prana as they fall upon every organism are returned from that organism according to the well-known laws of reflection. These rays, as is again well known, carry within themselves our pictures. Bearing these within them, they go up to the limit of the terrestrial prana noted above. It will be easy to conceive that within the imaginary sphere that surrounds our terrestrial prana, we now have a magnified picture of our central organism. Not one organism only, but all the smallest points, the most imperfect beginnings of organized life, as well as the most perfect organisms – all are pictured in this imaginary sphere. It is a magnificent picture-gallery; all that is seen or heard, touched, tasted or smelled on the face of the earth has a glorious and magnified picture there. At the limit of this terrestrial prana, the picture-forming tatwic rays exercise a double function.

Firstly they throw the sympathetic tatwic chords of the solar prana into similar motion. That is to say, these pictures are now consigned to the solar prana, from whence in due course they reach step by step to the universal intelligence itself.

Secondly, these rays react upon themselves, and turning back from the limiting sphere, are again reflected back to the center.

It is these pictures that the attentive mind sees in its noonday gaze into vacancy, and it is these pictures, seen in this mysterious way, that give us the finest food for our imagination and intellect, and supply us with a far-reaching clue to the nature and working of the laws that govern the life of the macrocosm and the microcosm. For these pictures tell us that the smallest of our actions, on whatever plane of our existence, actions that may be so insignificant to us as to pass unnoticed even by ourselves, are destined to receive an everlasting record, as the effect of the past and the cause of the future. These pictures again tell us of the existence of the five universal tatwas that play so important a part in the universe. It is these pictures that lead us to the discovery of the manifold constitution of man and the universe, and of those powers of the mind that have not yet received recognition at the hands of the official science of the day.

That these truths have found place in the Upanishad may be seen from the following quotation from the Ishopnishat, mantra 4:

"The Atma does not move: is one: is faster than the mind: the senses reach it not: as it is the foremost in motion. It goes beyond the others in rapid motion while itself at rest, in it the Recorder preserves the actions."

In the above quotation it is the word Matarishwa that I translate "Recorder". Ordinarily the word is translated as air, and so far as I know, the word has never been understood clearly in the sense of the "Recorder". My view, therefore, may be further explained with advantage.

The word is a compound of the words matari and swah. The word matari is the locative case of matri which ordinarily means mother, but which is rendered here as space, as the substratum of distance, from the root ma, to measure. The second word of the compound means the breather, coming as it does from the root Swas, to breathe. Hence the compound means "he who breathes in space". In explaining this word the commentator Sankaracharya goes on to say:

"The word 'Matarishwa', which has been derived as above, means the Vayu [the mover] which carries in it all the manifestations of prana, which is action itself, that which is the substratum of all the groups of causes and effects, and in which all the causes and effects are held like beads in a thread, that which is given the name of sutra [the thread] inasmuch as it holds in itself the whole of the world."

It is further said that the "actions" in the above quotation which this matarishwa holds in itself are all the movements of the individualized prana, as well as the actions of heating, lighting, ruining, etc., of the macrocosmic powers known as Agni, etc.

Now such a thing can by no means be the atmospheric air. It is evidently that phase of prana which acts as carrying the pictures of all actions, all motions from every point of space to every other point and to the limits of the surya mandala. This phase of prana is nothing more or less than the Recorder. It holds in itself forever and ever all the causes and effects, the antecedents and consequents of this world of ours.

It is action itself. This means that all action is a change of phase of prana.

It is said in the above quotation that this Recorder lives in the atma. Inasmuch as the atma exists, this Power always performs its function. The prana draws its life itself from the atma, and accordingly we find a similarity between the dualities of the two. It is said of the atma in the above extract that it does not move, and yet it moves faster than the mind.

These appear to be contradictory qualities at first sigh, and it is such qualities that make the ordinary God of commonplace theologians the absurd being he always looks to be. Let us, however, apply these qualities to prana, and once understood on this plane, they will be quite as clearly understood on the highest plane, the atma. It has been said more than once that from every point of the ocean of prana the tatwic rays fly in every direction, to every point within the surya mandala. Thus the ocean of prana is in eternal motion. For all this, however, does one point of this ocean ever change its place? Of course not. Thus while every point keeps its place, every point at the same time goes and shows itself in every other point.

It is the same simple way that the all-pervading atma is in eternal motion and yet always at rest.

The case is similar with all the planes of life; all our actions, all our thoughts, all our aspirations, receive an everlasting record in the books of Matarishwa.

I must now notice these pictures in a little more detail. The science of photography tells us that under certain conditions the visual pictures can be caught on the plane of the sensitive film. But how can we account for the reading of letters at a distance of 40 miles or more? Such phenomena are a matter of personal experience to me. Very recently, while sitting abstracted, or it may be in a kind of dream, about 4 o'clock in the morning, I read a postcard written by a friend to a friend about me, the very same night, at a distance of almost 30 miles. One more thing must be noticed here, I think. Almost half the card spoke about me, and the rest referred to other matters that might have a passing interest for me, but could not be engrossing. Now this rest of the card did not come before my eyes very clearly, and I felt that with all my effort I could not even keep my eye upon those lines or a sufficiently long time to understand them, but was irresistibly drawn towards the paragraph that spoke of me, and which I could read very clearly. Four days after this, the addressee showed it to me; it was exactly the same, sentence by sentence (so far as I could remember), as I had seen before. I mention this phenomenon in particular, as in it the various prerequisites for the production of these phenomena are clearly defined. We learn from an analysis of this incident the following facts:

(1) When he was writing, the writer of the card meant that I should read the card, and especially the paragraph that concerned me.

(2) I was very anxious to know the news about me that the card contained.

(3) In the frame of mind mentioned above my friend wrote the card. What happened? The picture of his thoughts on the card, both on the physical and the mental plane, flew in every direction along the tatwic rays of the macrocosmic prana and mind. A picture was immediately made on the macrocosmic spheres, and from thence it bent its rays towards the destination of the postcard. No doubt all minds in the earth received a shock of this current of thought at the same time. But my mind alone was sensitive to the card and the news it contained. It was, therefore, on my mind alone that any impression was made. The rays were, as it were, refracted into my mind, and the result described above followed.

It follows from this illustration that in order to receive the pictorial rays of the prana we must have a mind in a state of sympathy, and not of antipathy; that is to say, a mind free from all action or intense feeling for the time being is the fittest receptacle for the pictorial representations of the cosmos, and so for a correct knowledge of the past and the future. And if we have an intense desire to know the thing, so much the better for us. It is in this way that the divine occultist reads the records of the past in the book of nature, and it is on this road that the beginner of this science must walk according to the direction of our Guru.

It must be understood that everything in every aspect that has been or is being n our planet has a legible record in the book of nature, and the tatwic rays of the prana and the mind are constantly bringing the outlines of these pictures back to us. It is to a great extent due to this that the past never leaves us, but always lives within us, although many of its most magnificent monuments have been forever effaced from the face of our planet for the ordinary gaze. These returning rays are always inclined toward the center that originally gave them birth. In the case of the mineral surroundings of terrestrial phenomena these centers are pre-served intact for ages upon ages, and it is quite possible for any sensitive mind, at any time, to turn these rays towards itself by coming into contact with any material remains of historic phenomena. A stone unearthed at Pompeii is pictured as part of the great event that destroyed the city, and the rays of that picture naturally are inclined towards that piece of stone. If Mrs. Denton puts the stone to her forehead, a sympathetic and receptive condition is the only pre-requisite for the transference of the whole picture to her mind. This sympathetic state of mind may be natural to a person, or it may be acquired. It may be mentioned that what we are in the habit of calling natural powers are really acquired, but they have been acquired in previous incarnations. Shiva says:

"There are some to whom the tatwas become known, when the mind is purified by habituation, either by the acquired velocity of other births or by the kindness of the Guru."

It seems that two pieces of granite, the same to all intents and purposes externally, may have an entirely different tatwic color, for the color of a thing depends to a very great extent upon its tatwic surrounding. It is this occult color that constitutes the real soul of things, although the reader must by this time know that the Sanskrit word prana is more appropriate.

It is no myth to say that the practiced yogi might bring the picture of any part of the world, past or present, before his mind's eye with a single effort of his will. And not only visual pictures, as our illustration might lead the reader to think. The preservation and formation of visual pictures is only the work of the luminiferous ether, the taijas tatwa. The other tatwas perform their functions as well. The akasa or soniferous ether preserves all the sounds that have ever been heard or are being heard on earth, and similarly the remaining three other preserve the records of the remaining sensations. We see, therefore, that combining all these pictures, a yogi in contemplation might have before his mind's eye any man at any distance whatsoever and might hear his voice also. Glyndon, in Italy, seeing and hearing the conversation of Viola and Zanoni in their distant home, is therefore not merely a dream of the poet; it is a scientific reality. The only thing necessary is to have a sympathetic mind. The phenomena of mental telepathy, psychometry, clairvoyance and clairaudience, are all phases of this tatwic action. Once understood, it is all a very simple affair. It may be useful in this place to offer some reflections as to how these pictorial representations of a man's present go to shape his future. I shall first attempt to show how complete the record is. At the outset I may remind the reader of what I have said about the tatwic color of everything. It is this that gives individuality even to a piece of stone.

This pictorial whole is only the cosmic counterpart of the individual prana maya kosha (the coil of life). It is possible that anyone who may not have thoroughly understood the manner of the storing up of tatwic energy in the individual prana may more easily comprehend the phenomena in its cosmic counterpart. In fact, the macrocosmic and microcosmic phenomena are both links of the same chain, and both will conduce to the thorough understanding of the whole. Suppose a man stands on a mountain, with the finest prospect of nature stretched out before his eyes. As he stands there contemplating this wealth of beauty, his picture in this posture is at once made in the ecliptic. Not only is his external; appearance pictured, but the hue of is life receives the fullest representation. If the agni tatwa prevails in him at that moment, if there is the light of satisfaction in his face, if the look in his eyes is calm, collected and pleasant, if he is so much absorbed in the gaze as to forget everything else, tatwas separate or in composite will do their duty, and all the satisfaction, calmness, pleasure, attention or inattention will be represented to the finest degree in the sphere of the ecliptic. If he walks or runs, comes down or jumps up or forward, the tatwic rays of prana picture the generating and the generated colors with the utmost faithfulness in the same retentive sphere.

A man stands with a weapon in his hand, with the look of cruelty in his eye, with the glow of inhumanity in his veins, his victim, man or animal, helpless or struggling before him. The whole phenomenon is instantly recorded. There stands the murderer and the victim in their truest possible colors, there is the solitary room or the jungle, the dirty shed or the filthy slaughterhouse; all are there as surely and certainly as they are in the eye of the murderer r the victim himself.

Let us again change the scene. We have a liar before us. He tells a lie, and thereby injures some brother man. No sooner is the word uttered than the akasa sets to work with all possible activity. There we have the most faithful representation. The liar is there from the reflection that the thought if the injured person throws into the individual prana; there is the injured man also. The words are there with all the energy of the contemplated wrong. And if that contemplated wrong is completed, there is also the change for the worse that his mendacity has produced in the victim. There is nothing of the surroundings, the antecedent and the consequent postures – the causes and effects – that is not represented there.

The scene changes, and we come to a thief. Let the night be as dark as it may, let the thief be a circumspect and wary as he can; our picture is there with all its colors well defined, though perhaps not so prominent. The time, the house, the wall, the sleeping and injured inmates, the stolen property, the subsequent day, the sorrowful householders, with all the antecedent and consequent postures, are pictured. And this is not only for the murderer, the thief, or the liar, but for the adulterer, the forger, the villain who thinks his crime is hidden from every human eye. Their deeds, like all deeds that have ever been done, are vividly, clearly, exactly recorded in nature's picture gallery. Instances might be multiplied, but it is unnecessary. What has been said is sufficient to explain the principle, and the application is useful and not very difficult. But now we must bring our pictures back from our gallery.

We have seen that time and space and all the possible factors of a phenomenon receive an accurate representation there, and these tatwic rays are united to the time that saw them leaving their record on the plane of our pictorial region. When, in the course of ages, the same Time throws its shade again upon the earth, the pictorial rays, stored up long since, energize man-producing matter, and shape it according to their own potential energy, which now begins to become active. It will be readily conceded that the sun dives life to the earth – to men as well as to vegetables and minerals. Solar life takes human shape in the womb of the mother, and this is only an infusion of some one set of our pictorial rays into the sympathetic life that already shows itself on our planet. These rays thus produce for themselves a gross human body in the womb of the mother, and then having the now somewhat different and differing maternal body, start on their terrestrial journey. As time advances, the pictorial representation changes it tatwic postures, and with it the gross body does the same.

In the case of the rebirth of the man we saw gazing on the mountains, the calm, watchful, contented attitude of the mind that he cultivated then has its influence upon the organism now, and once more the man enjoys the beauty of nature and so is pleased and happy.

But now take the case of the cruel murderer. He is by nature cruel, and he still yearns to murder and destroy, and he could not be restrained from his horrible practices; but the picture of the ebbing life of his victim is now part and parcel of his constitution, the pain, the terror, and the feeling of despair and helplessness are there in all their strength. Occasionally he feels as if the blood of life were leaving his very veins. There is no apparent cause, and yet he suffers pain; he is subject to unaccountable fits of terror, despair and helplessness. His life is miserable; slowly but surely it wanes away.

Let the curtain fall on this stage. The incarnated thief now comes on the stage. His friends leave him one by one or he is driven away from them. The picture of the lonely house must assert its power over him. He is doomed to a lonely house. The picture of somebody coming into the house through some unfrequented part and stealing some of his property, makes its appearance with the fullest strength. The man is doomed to eternal cowardice. He draws towards himself the same grief and heart-rending that he caused to others long ago. This posture of heart-rending grief has its influence upon him in the ordinary way, and it creates its surrounding under the same influence.

These illustrations are sufficient to explain the law according to which these cosmic pictures govern our future lives. Whatever other sins may be committed under the innumerable circumstance of life, their tatwic effects can be traced easily through the pictorial representations of the cosmos.

It is not difficult to understand that the picture of each individual organism upon the face of the earth is pictured in prana, and it is these pictures, in my opinion, that correspond to the ideas of Plato on the highest plane of existence. A very interesting question arises at this point. Are these pictures of eternal existence, or do they only come into existence after formations have taken place on the terrestrial plane? Ex nihilo nihil fit is a well-known doctrine of philosophy, and I hold with Vyasa that the representations (what we now call pictures) of all objects in their generic, specific, and individual capacities have been existing forever in the universal mind. Swara, or what may be called the Breath of God, the Breath of Life, is nothing more or less than abstract intelligence, as has been explained, or intelligent motion, if such an expression is better understood. Our book says:

"In the swara are pictured, or represented, the Vedas and the Sastras, in the swara the highest Gandharvas, and in the swara all the three worlds; the swara is atma itself."

It is not necessary to enter more thoroughly into a discussion of this problem; the suggestion is sufficient. It might be said, however, that all formation in progress on the face of our planet is the assuming by everything under the influence of solar ideas of the shape of these ideas. The process is quite similar to the process of wet earth taking impressions of anything that is pressed upon it. The idea of anything is its soul.

Human souls (prana maya kosha) exist in this sphere just like the souls of other things, and are affected in that home of theirs by terrestrial experience in the manner mentioned above.

In the course of ages, these ideas make their appearance in the physical plane again and again, according to the laws hinted at previously.

I have also said that these pictures have their counterparts in the mental and the higher atmospheres. Now it might be said that just as these solar pictures recur again and again, there are times at which these mental pictures also recur. The ordinary deaths known to us are terrestrial deaths. This means to say that the influence of the solar pictures is withdrawn for some time from the earth. After some time, the duration depending upon the colors of the picture, they throw their influence again upon the earth, and we have terrestrial rebirth. We may die any number of terrestrial deaths, and yet our solar life might not be extinct.

But men of the present manwantara might die solar deaths under certain circumstances. Then they pass out of the influence of the sun and are born again only in the region of the second Manu. Men who now die solar deaths will remain in the state of bliss all through the present manwantara. Their rebirth might also be delayed for more than one manwantara. All these pictures remain in the bosom of Manu during the manwantarapralaya. In the same way, men might undergo higher deaths, and pass their time in a state of even higher and more enduring bliss. The mental coil may be broken, too, just as the gross, the terrestrial, and the solar might be, and then the blessed soul remains in bliss and unborn until the dawn of the second day of Brahma. Higher still and longer still is the state that follows Brahmic death. Then the spirit is at rest for the remaining Kalpa and the Mahapralaya that follows. After this it will be easy to understand the meaning of the Hindu doctrine, that during the night of Brahma the human soul and the whole of the universe is hidden in the bosom of Brahma like the tree in the seed.

XI. *The Manifestations of Psychic Force*

Psychic Force is the form of matter known as vijnana in active connection with the mental and life matters. In the quotation given above from the Ishnopnishat, it has been said that the deva – the macrocosmic and microcosmic manifestations of prana – do not reach the atma, inasmuch as it moves faster than even the mind. The tatwas of prana move with a certain momentum. The mind has greater velocity, and psychic matter greater still. In the presence of the higher, the lower plane always appears to be at rest, and is always amenable to its influence. Creation is a manifestation of the various macrocosmic spheres with their various centers. In each of these spheres – the prana, the manas, and the vijnana– the universal tatwic rays give birth to innumerable individualities on their own planes. Each truti on the plane of prana is a life-coil (prana maya kosha). The rays that give existence to each of these truti come from each and all of the other truti, which are situated in the space allotted to each of the five tatwas and their innumerable admixtures, and which represent therefore all the possible tatwic manifestations of life.

On the plane of manas each mental truti represents an individual mind. Each individual mind is given birth to by mental tatwic rays from the other quarter. These rays came from all the other truti situated under the dominion of each of the five tatwas and their innumerable admixtures and representing therefore all the possible tatwic phases of mental life.

On the psychic plane, each truti represents an individual soul brought into existence by the psychic tatwas flying from every point to every other point. These rays come from every truti situated under the dominion of each of the five tatwas and their innumerable admixtures, and thus representing all the possible manifestations of psychic life.

The latter class of truti on the various planes of existence are the so-called gods and goddesses. The former class are coils that manifest themselves in earthly life.

Each psychic truti is thus a little reservoir of every possible tatwic phase of life that might manifest itself on the lower planes of existence. And so, sending its rays downward just like the sun, these truti manifest themselves in the truti of the lower planes. According to the prevalent phase of tatwic color in these three sets of truti, the vijana (psychic) selects its mind, the mind selects its coil, and in the end the life-coil creates its habitation in the earth.

The first function of the individual truti vijana is to sustain in the life of the mental truti just as the macrocosmic vijana sustains the life of the macrocosmic mind. And so also does the mental truti sustain the life of the individual truti of prana. In this state, the souls are conscious only of their subjectivity with reference to the mind and the prana. They know that they sustain the lower truti, they know themselves, they know all the other psychic truti, and they know the whole of the macrocosm of Iswara, the tatwic rays reflecting every point into their indvidual con-sciousness. They are omniscient; they are perfectly happy because they are perfectly balanced.

When the prana maya kosha enters the habitation of earth, the soul is assailed by finitude for the first time. This means a curtailment, or rather the creation of a new curtailed consciousness. For long ages the soul takes no note of these finite sensations, but as the impressions gain greater and greater strength they are deluded into a belief of identity with these finite impressions. From absolute subjectivity consciousness is transferred to relative passivity. A new world of appearances is created. This is their fall. How these sensations and perceptions, etc., are born, and how they affect the soul, already has been discussed. How the soul is awakened out of this forgetfulness and what it does then to liberate itself will come further on.

It will be seen at this stage that the soul lives two lives, an active and a passive. In the active capacity it goes on governing and sustaining the substantial life of the lower truti. In the passive capacity it forgets itself and deludes itself into identity with the changes of the lower truti imprinted upon them by the external tatwas. The consciousness is transferred to finite phases.

The whole fight of the soul upon reawakening consists in the attempt to do away with its passive capacity and regain this pristine purity. This fight is yoga, and the powers that yoga evokes in the mind and the prana are nothing more than tatwic manifestations of the psychic force, calculated to destroy the power of the external world on the soul. This constant change of phase in the new unreal finite coils of existence is the upward march of the life current from the beginnings of relative consciousness to the original absolute state.

There is no difficulty in understanding the how of these manifestations. They are there in the psychic reservoir, and they simply show themselves when the lower trutis assume the state of sympathetic polish and tatwic inclination. Thus the spectrum only shows itself when certain objects assume the polish and form of a prism.

Ordinarily the psychic force does not manifest itself either in the prana or the mind in any uncommon phase. Humanity progresses as a whole, and whatever manifestations of this force take place, they take in races as a whole. Finite minds are therefore slow to recognize it.

But all the individuals of a race do not have the same strength of tatwic phase. Some show greater sympathy with the psychic force in one or more of its component tatwic phases. Such organisms are called mediums. In them the particular tatwic phase of psychic force with which they are in greater sympathy than the rest of their mind, makes its uncommon appearance. This difference of individual sympathy is caused by a difference of degree in the commissions and omission of different individuals, or by the practice of yoga.

In this way, this psychic force might manifest itself in the shape of all the innumerable possibilities of tatwic combination. So far as theory is concerned, these manifestations might cover the whole domain of tatwic manifestations in the visible macrocosm (and also in the invisible, which, however, we do not know). These manifestations may violate all our present notions of time and space, cause and effect, force and matter.

Intelligently utilized, this force might very well perform the functions of the vril of "The Coming Race". The following essays will trace some of these manifestations on the plane of the mind.

XII. Yoga -- The Soul (I)

I have described two principles of the human constitution: prana and manas. Something also has been said about the nature and relations of the soul. The gross body was omitted as needing no special handling.

The five manifestations of each of the two principles (the prana and the manas), it may be mentioned, may be either fortunate or unfortunate. Those manifestations are fortunate which are consonant with our true culture, which lead us to our highest spiritual development, the summum bonum of humanity. Those that keep us chained to the sphere of recurring births and deaths may be called unfortunate. On each of the two planes of life (prana and manas) there is a possibility of double existence. We might have a fortunate and an unfortunate prana, a happy and an unhappy mind. Considering these two to be four, the number of principles of the human constitution might be raised from five to seven. The unhappy intelligences of the one plane ally themselves with the unhappy ones of the other, the happy ones with the happy, and we have in the human constitution an arrangement of principles something like the following:

(1) The gross body (sthula sarira), (2) the unhappy prana, (3) the unhappy mind, (4) the happy prana, (5) the happy mind, (6) the soul (vijana), and (7) the spirit (ananda).

The fundamental division in the fivefold division is upadhi, the particular and distinct state of matter (prakriti) in each case; in the sevenfold division it is the nature of Karma with reference to its effect upon human evolution.

Both the sets of these powers, the blessed and the unhappy, work upon the same plane, and although the blessed manifestations tend in the long run towards the state of moksha, that state is not reached unless and until the higher powers (the siddhi) are induced in the mind by the exercise of yoga. Yoga is a power of the soul. Therefore it is necessary to say something about the soul and Yoga before the higher powers of the mind can be intelligibly described. Yoga is the science of human culture in the highest sense of the word. Its purpose is the purification and strengthening of the mind. By its exercise is filled with high aspirations, and acquires divine powers, while the unhappy tendencies die out.

The second and third principles are burnt up by the fire of divine knowledge, and the state of what is called salvation in life is attained. By and bye the fourth principle too becomes neutralized, and the soul passes into a state of manwantaric moksha. The soul may pass higher still according to the strength of her exercise. When the mind too is at rest, as in sound sleep (sushupti) during life, the omniscience of the vijnana is reached. There is still a higher state: the state of ananda. Such are the results of yoga. I must now describe the nature of the thing and the process of acquirement.

So far as the nature of Yoga is concerned, I may say that mankind has reached its present state of development by the exercise of this great power. Nature herself is a great Yogi, and humanity has been, and is being, purified into perfection by the exercise of her sleepless will. Man need only imitate the great teacher to shorten the road to perfection for his individual self. How are we to render ourselves fit for that great imitation? What are the steps on the great ladder of perfection? These things have been discovered for us by the great sages of yore, and Patanjali's little book is only a short and suggestive transcript of so much of our past experiences and future potentialities as is recorded in the book of nature. This little book uses the word Yoga in a double signification. The first is a state of the mind otherwise called samadhi; the second is a set of acts and observances that induce that state in the mind. The definition given by the sage is a negative one, and is applicable only on the plane of the mind. The source of the positive power lies in the higher principle; the soul Yoga (it is said) is the keeping in check of the five manifestations of the mind. The very wording of the definition is involved in the supposition of the existence of a power that can control and keep the mental manifestations in check. This power is familiar to us as freedom of the will. Although the soul is deluded by the manifestations of egoism (asmita) on the mental plane into regarding herself as a slave of the second and third principles, that is not the fact, and the awakening takes place as soon as the chord of egoism is slackened to a certain extent. This is the first step in the initiation by nature herself of the race of man. It is a matter of necessity. The side-by-side working with each

other of the second and third and the fourth and fifth principles weakens the hold of natural mental asmita upon the soul. "I am these, or of these mental manifestations", says Egoism. Such a state of affairs, however, cannot last long. These manifestations are double in

nature; the one is just the reverse of the other. Which of them is one

with the ego: the unhappy or the blessed? No sooner is this question asked
than the awakening takes place. It is impossible to answer any of these
questions in the affirmative, and the soul naturally ends in discovering
that she is a separate thing from the mind, and that although she has
been the slave, she might be (what she naturally is) the Lord of the mind.
Up to this time the soul has been tossed this way or that in obedience to
the tatwic vibrations of the mind. Her blind sympathy with the mental
manifestations gives her unison with the mind, and hence the tossing. The
chord of sympathy is loosened by the waking. The stronger the nature,
the greater the departure from unison. Instead of the soul being tossed
by the mental vibrations, it is now time that the mind should vibrate in
obedience to the vibrations of the soul. This assumption of lordship is the
freedom of the will, and this obedience of the mind to the vibrations of
the soul is Yoga. The manifestations evoked in the mind by the external
tatwas must now give way to the stronger motion coming from the soul.
By and bye the mental colors change their very nature, and the mind
comes to coincide with the soul. In other words, the individual mental
principle is neutralized, and the soul is free in her omniscience.

Let us now trace the acquirements of the mind step by step up to
samadhi.

Samadhi, or the mental state induced by the practice of Yoga, has two
descriptions. As long as the mind is not perfectly absorbed in the soul
the state is called samprajnata. That is the state in which the discovery
of new truths follows labor in every department of nature. The second
is the state of perfect mental absorption. It is called asamprajnata. In
this there is no knowing, no discovering of unknown things. It is a state
of intuitive omniscience. Two questions are naturally suggested at the
awakening stage:

"If I am these manifestations, which of them am I? I think I am none
of them. What am I then? What are these?"

The second question is solved in the samprajnata samadhi, the first
in the other. Before entering further into the nature of samadhi, a word
about habituation and apathy. These two are mentioned by Patanjali as the
two means of checking mental manifestation, and it is very important to
understand them thoroughly The manifestation of apathy is the reflection
in the mind of the color of the soul when she becomes aware of her free
nature and consequently is disgusted at the mastery of the passions. It is
a necessary consequence of the awakening. Habituation is the repetition
of the state so as to confirm it in the mind.

The confirmation of the mind in this state means a state of ordinary mental inactivity. By this I mean that the five ordinary manifestations are at rest for the first time. This being so, the mind is for the time being left free to receive any influences. Here for the first time we see the influence of the soul in the shape of curiosity (Vitarka). What is this? What is that? How is this? How is that? This is the form in which curiosity shows itself in the mind. Curiosity is a desire to know, and a question is a manifestation of such a desire. But how does man become familiar with questions? The mental shape of curiosity and question will be understood easily by paying a little attention to the remarks I have made on the genesis of desire. The process of the birth of philosophical curiosity is similar to that of the birth of desire. In the latter the impulse comes from the external world through Prana, and in the former, directly from the soul. The place of pleasure in this is supplied by the reflection into the mind of the knowledge of the soul that self and independence are better than non- self and the enslaving cords thereof. The strength of the philosophical curiosity depends upon the strength of this reflection, and as this reflection is rather faint in the beginning (as it generally is in the present state of the spiritual development), the hold of philosophical curiosity upon the mind bears almost no comparison in strength with the hold of desire.

Philosophical curiosity is then the first step of mental ascent towards Yoga. To begin with, we place before our mind every possible manifestation of nature, and try to fit in every possible phase of it with every related manifestation. In plain language, it is to apply ourselves to the investigation of all the branches of natural science one by one.

This is the natural result of curiosity. By this attempt to discover the relations already existing or possible, essential or potential, among the phenomena of nature, another power is induced in the mind. Patanjali calls this power vichara, meditation. The radical idea of the word is to go among the various relations of the portions that make up the whole subject of our contemplation. It is only a deeper hold on the mind of the philosophical curiosity noticed above. The third state of this samadhi is what is called ananda, happiness or bliss. As long as there is curiosity or meditation, the mind is only assuming the consistency of the soul. This means to say that as yet the vibrations of the soul are only making way into the mind; they have not yet entirely succeeded. When the third stage is arrived at, however, the mind is sufficiently polished to receive the full and clear image of the sixth coil. The mind is conscious of this image as bliss. Every man who has devoted himself to the study of nature has been in that coveted state for however short a time. It is very difficult to make it intelligible by description, but I am sure that the majority of my readers are not strangers to it.

But whence does this bliss come? What is it? I have called it a reflection of the soul. But first of all, what is the soul? From what I have written up to this time, the reader will no doubt surmise that I understand the soul to be only a picture of the gross body, the prana, and the mind, so far only as its constitution is concerned.

I have mentioned that in the macrocosm the sun is in the center, the prana the atmosphere of the second principle, and that the ecliptic marks the shape of this principle. I have also mentioned that the individual human principle is only a picture of this macrocosmic whole. I have mentioned again that in the macrocosm virat is the center and manu the atmosphere of second principle. This atmosphere is made of the five universal tatwas, just like prana, the only difference being that the mental tatwas undergo a greater number of vibrations per second than the tatwas of prana. I have also said that the individual mind is an exact picture of the macrocosmic mind, the aspect differing with the surroundings of time, just as in the case of prana.

Now I have to say the same with regard to the soul. In the macrocosm there is Brahma for the center, and vijana for the atmosphere of this principle. As the earth moves in prana, as the sun moves in manu, as the manu (or virat) breathes in vijana, so the soul breathes in the highest atmosphere of ananda. Brahma is the center of spiritual life, as the sun is the center of prana, and virat the center of mental life. These centers are similar in luminosity to the sun, but ordinary senses cannot perceive them because the number of tatwic vibrations per second is beyond their power.

The soul of the universe (the vijana maya kosha), with Brahma for its center, is our psychic ideal.

The tatwic wires of this sphere extend over what we call a Brahmanda. This they do in a way similar to the tatwic rays of prana with which we are familiar through the medium of gross matter. This center with this universe forms the self-conscious universe. All the lower centers exist within the bosom of this atmosphere.

Under the influence of gross matter the mental macrocosm registers the external pictures; that is to say, it gains the power of manifesting itself in the five ways I have described in the essay on mind. Under the Brahma, however, the mental macrocosm (Manu) attains the higher powers under discussion. This double influence changes, after a time, the nature of Manu itself. The universe has, as it were, a new mind after every manwantara. This change is always for the better. The mind is ever spiritualizing. The later the Manu the more spiritual. A time will come when the present macrocosmic mind will be entirely absorbed into the soul. The same is the case with the microcosm of man. Thus Brahma is by nature omniscient. He is conscious of a self. The types of everything that was or is to be in the process of time are but so many varying compositions of his tatwas. Every phase of the universe, with its antecedents and consequents, is in him. It is himself, his own self- consciousness. One mind is absorbed in him in the space of fourteen manwantara. The motion of the mental tatwas is so much accelerated that they become spiritual. By the time that this takes place in the Universe the vibrations of the tatwas of prana too are being accelerated under the influence of Manu until the prana itself is turned into the Manu of the next period. And again, while this is being done, the gross matter is similarly developing itself into prana.

This is the process of involution, but for the present let us leave it here and resume the subject.

The human soul is an exact picture of this macrocosmic principle. It is omniscient like its prototype, and has the same constitution. But the omniscience of the human soul is yet latent on account of her forgetfulness. The sixth principle (absolute) has developed only a little. Humanity in general has only a very dim notion of infinity, of Godhead, and of all such subjects. This means that the rays of the infinite are only just evoking our sixth principle into active life at this stage of our progress. When in the process of time the rays of the infinite gather sufficient strength, our soul will come out in her true light. We might accelerate this process by vairagya (apathy), which gives strength to Yoga, as we have seen.

The means of strengthening Yoga deserve separate consideration. Some of them help to remove those influences and forces that are antagonistic to progress; others, such as the contemplation of the divine principle, accelerate the process of development of the human soul, and the consequent absorption of the mind in the soul. At present I have simply to discover the nature of the blissful samadhi, which I spoke of as being caused by the reflection of the soul in the mind.

This reflection simply means the assumption by the mind of the state of the soul. The mind passes from its own ordinary state to the state of the higher energy of the soul. The greater number of tatwic vibrations per second make their way in the matter of a lower number of tatwic vibrations per second. The English language recognizes this rising up of the mind, this passing out of itself, as elation, and this is the meaning of the word ananda as qualifying the third state of the samprajnata samadhi. The ananda maya kosha takes its name from its being the state of the highest upheaval. Every moment of ananda is a step towards the absorption of the mind as it changes its nature, passing forever into a higher state of consistency. That state which in ananda only appeared in the moment of triumph now becomes part and parcel of the mind. This confirmation of the higher energy is known by the name of Asmita, which may be translated by the word egoism, but means making part and parcel of self.

XIII. Yoga (II)

The object in view in this article is to mark the stages along the road of mental matter to its final absorption in the soul. In the last essay I brought the mind to the state of samprajnata samadhi. It is in this state that the mind acquires the power of discovering new truths, and seeing new combinations of things existent. As this state has been attained in the long cycle of bygone ages, man has acquired a knowledge of science to its present stage of development, and the attainment of this quantum of knowledge has been the means of raising our minds to our present pitch of perfection, when we have learned to say that these great powers are native to the human mind. As I have shown, these powers have become native to the mind only after long submission of the mind to the influence of the soul.

By the constant exercise of this samadhi the mind learns to incline towards those cosmic influences that are in their very nature antagonistic to those bad powers of our constitution that check our progress. These powers tend to die out naturally. The ultimate goal of this march is that the state of mind when its manifestation become entirely potential. The soul, if she pleases, might propel them by her inherent power into the domain of the actual, but they lose all power to draw the soul after them.

When this state is reached, or when it is about to be reached, certain powers begin to show themselves in the mind, which in the present cycle are by no means common. This state is technically called paravairagya, or the Higher Apathy.

The word vairagya usually is rendered into English as apathy, and is looked upon with disfavor by modern thinkers. This is, I believe, owing to a misconception of the meaning of the word. It is generally understood that misanthropy is the only indication, or perhaps the highest perfection, of this mental state. Nothing can be further from the intention of those sages who put vairagya down as the highest means of the attainment of bliss. Vairagya or apathy is defined by Vyasa in his commentary on The Aphorisms of Yoga as the "final state of perfected knowledge". It is that state in which the mind, coming to know the real nature of things, would no longer be deluded into false pleasure by the manifestations of avidya. When this upward inclination becomes confirmed, when this habit of soaring towards the divine becomes second nature, the name of paravairagya is given to the complementary mental state.

This state is reached in many ways, and the road is marked by many clearly defined stages. One way is the practice of samprajnata samadhi. By the constant practice of this samadhi, to which the mind runs of itself when it once tastes the bliss of the fourth stage of that state, the mind is habituated to a state of faith in the efficacy of the pursuit. This faith is nothing more than a state of mental lucidity in which the yet unknown truths of nature begin to throw their shadows before them. The mind begins to feel truth in any and every place, and drawn by the taste of bliss (ananda), sets to work out the process of its evolution with greater and greater zeal. This faith has been called Sraddha by Patanjali, and he calls the consequent zeal Virya.

Confirmed in this zeal and working on, the manifestation of memory comes in naturally. This is a high state of evolution. Every truth becomes present before the mind's eye at the slightest thought, and the four stages of samadhi make their appearance again and again till the mind becomes very nearly a mirror of Nature.

This corresponds to the state of paravairagya, which in the second place would also be attained by the contemplation of the High Prototype of the Soul. This is the Iswara of Ptanjali, the macrocosmic soul that remains forever in that entity's soul of pristine purity. It is this Iswara of that I have spoken as the self-conscious universe.

This Iswara, as I conceive it, is only a macrocosmic center, similar in nature to the sun, though higher in function.

As the sun with his ocean of Prana is the prototype of our life-principle, prana maya kosha, so Iswara is the great prototype of our souls. What is the sixth principle of not only a phase of the existence of this great being prolonged as a separate phase into the lower principles, yet destined to emerge again into its own true self? Just as I have shown that the principles of life live in the sun after our terrestrial death, to recur again and again into actual life, so too the soul lives in the Iswara in a similar fashion. We may look upon this entity as being the group of all the liberated souls, but at the same time we must remember that the unliberated souls also are his undeveloped reflections, destined in the long run to attain their original state. It is therefore necessary to assume the independent existence of

Iswara, and of other souls in Iswara.

This macrocosmic psychic center, this ideal of the sixth principle in man, is the great reservoir of every actual force in the universe. He is the true type of the perfection of the human soul. The incidents of mental and physical existence which, however perfect in themselves, are to His more comprehensive nature mere imperfections, find no place in Him. There is no misery for Him – the five comprehensive miseries of Patanjali are enumerated above – for misery can arise only in the retrograde process of the first awakening of the mind, only being caused by sensation, and the human sixth principle not yet gaining sufficient strength in the process of time to draw the mind towards itself and out of the domain of the senses, to make it what its prototype originally is, the rod of dominion, and not as sensation has made it, the instrument of slavery.

By this conemplation of the sixth principle of the Universe, a sympathy is established naturally between it and the human soul. That sympathy is only necessary for the Universal Tatwic Law to work with greater effect. The human soul begins to be cleansed of the dust of the world and in its turn affects the mind in a similar way, and therein the yogi becomes conscious of this influence by the slackening of the fetters forged by Prakriti, and a daily, hourly strengthening of heavenward aspirations.

The human soul then begins to become a center of power for its own little universe, just as Iswara is the center of power in His universe. The microcosm then becomes a perfect little picture of the macrocosm. When perfection is attained, all the mental and physiological tatwas of the microcosm, and to a certain extent of the surrounding world, become the slaves of the soul. Whitherso it may incline, the tatwas are at its back. He may will, and the atmospheric Vayu tatwa, with any amount of strength he pleases or is capable of centering, will set in motion any piece of furniture within the reach of his will. He may will, and at the instant the apas tatwa will slake your thirst, cure your fever, or in fact wash off the germs of any disease. He may will, and any and every tatwa on either of the lower planes will do its work for him. These high powers do not wait to come in all of a sudden, but show themselves gradually, and according to the special aptitudes in special forms.

But a description of these powers is not my present business. My only purpose is to show in what way, according to the universal law of nature, by contemplation of the macrocosmic sixth principle, that the human soul becomes the means for the mind attaining the state called paravairagya.

Besides these two, the author of The Aphorisms of Yoga enumerates five more ways in which the minds of those who are already by the power of previous karma inclined towards the divine, are seen to work out their way to the sate of paravairagya.

This first way is the habituating of the mind to the manifestations of pleasure, sympathy, elation, and pity toward the comfortable, the miserable, and the vicious respectively. Every good man will tell us that the manifestation of joy at the comfort of another is a high virtue. Why, what harm is there in jealousy? I think no other science except the philosophy of the tatwas explains with any amount of satisfaction the reason why of such questions.

We have seen that in a state of enjoyment, comfort, pleasure, satisfaction, and the like, the prithivi or the apas tatwa prevails in the prana and the mind. It is evident that if we put our minds in the same, we induce either of the two tatwas in our life and mental principles. What will be the result? A process of purification will set in. Both the principles will being to be cleansed of any trace of defect that the excess of any remaining tatwas may have given to our constitution.

All those physiological or mental causes that induce inattention in the mind are removed. Bodily distempers take their leave for they are the result of the disturbance of the balance of the physiological tatwas, and comfort, pleasure and enjoyment are foreign to these. The one induces the other. As the balance of the tatwas brings comfort and enjoyment of life, so the sense of comfort and enjoyment that colors our prana and mind when we put ourselves in sympathy with the comfortable, restores the balance of our tatwas.

And when the balance of tatwas is restored, what remains? Disinclination to work, doubt, laziness and other feelings of that kind can no longer stand, and the only result is the restoration of the mind to perfect calmness. As Vyasa says in his commentary, the White Law makes its appearance in the mind. Such and in a similar way is the result of the manifestation of the other qualities. But for such a result to beachieved, there must be long and powerful application.

The next method is Pranayama, deep expiration and inspiration. This too conduces to the same end and in the same way. The drawing of deep breaths in and out has to some extent the same effect as running and other hard exercise. The heat that is produced burns down certain elements of disease, which if it desirable should be burnt. But the practice in its effects differs for the better from hard exercise. In hard exercise the susumna begins to play, and that is not good for physiological health. Pranayama, if properly performed, however, is beneficial from a physiological as well as from a mental point of view. The first effect that is produced in pranayama is the general prevalence of the prithivi tatwa. It is unnecessary to remind the reader that the apas tatwa carries the breath lowest down, and that the Prithivi is the next. In our attempt to draw deeper breaths than usual, the prithivi tatwa cannot but be introduced, and the general prevalence of this tatwa, with the consequent golden tinge of the circle of light round our heads, can never fail to cause fixity of purpose and strength of attention. The apas tatwa comes in next. This is the silvery hue of innocence that encircles the head of a saint and marks the attainment of paravairagya.

The next is the attainment of the two-fold lucidity – the sensuous and the cardiac. The sensuous lucidity is the power of the senses to perceive the changes of prana. The previously trained attention, according to special aptitudes, is centered on any one of the five senses or more. If centered in the eyes, one can see the physiological and atmospheric colors of prana. I can affirm this by personal experience. I can see the various colors of the seasons. I can see the rain coming an hour, two hours, and sometimes even two days before an actual shower. Bright sheets of the green washed into coolness and purity by the white make their appearance anywhere about me – in the room, in the heavens, on the table before me, on the wall in front. When this happens, I am sure that rain is in the air and will come down soon. If the green is streaked with red, it takes some time to come, but it is surely preparing.

These remarks are enough for color. The power can be made to show itself by a sustained attempt to look into space, or anything else, as the moon, a star, a jewel, and so on. The remaining four senses also attain similar powers, and sounds, smells, tastes and touches that ordinary humanity cannot perceive begin to be perceived by the Yogi.

The cardiac lucidity is the power of the mind to feel and also that of the senses to perceive thoughts. In the article on Prana, I have given a chart of the head, specifying the places and giving the colors of the various kinds of mental manifestations. These colors are seen by anyone who has or acquires the power, and they constitute the surest book in which to read the thoughts of any man. By sustained practice one will recognize the finest shades.

One can also feel these thoughts. The modifications of thought moving along the universal tatwic wires affect any and every man. They each impart a distinct impulse to the prana maya kosha, and thus a distinguishable impulse to the throbs of the brain and the more easily perceivable throbs of the heart. A man who studies these throbs of the heart and sits with his attention centered into the heart (while it is of course open to every influence) learns to feel every influence there. The effect on the heart of the mental modifications of other people is a fact that, so far as quality is concerned, may be verified by the commonest experience.

This sensuous or cardiac lucidity, as the case may be, once attained kills skepticism, and in the end conduces to the state of paravairagya.

In the next place, says Patanjali, one may rely upon the knowledge obtainable through dreams and sleep. But this will do for the present.

XIV. Yoga – The Soul (III)

The five ethereal currents of sensation are focused in the brain, and motion is transmitted to the mental principle from these five centers of force. These various foci serve a connecting links between the mental and the life-principles. The visual currents produce in the mind the capability of becoming conscious of color. In other words, they produce eyes in the mind. Similarly, the mind gets the capability of receiving the impressions of the four remaining sensations. This capability is acquired after the exposure of ages. Cycles upon cycles pass, and the mind is not yet capable of receiving these tatwic vibrations. The wave of life begins its organized journey upon earth with vegetable forms. Since that time external currents begin to affect the vegetable organism, and this is the beginning of what we call sensation. The modifications of the external tatwas through the individualized vegetable life strike the chords of the latent mind, but it will not yet respond. It is not in sympathy. Higher and higher through vegetable forms the life-wave travels; greater and greater is the force with which it strikes the mental chords, and better and better is the capability of that principle to respond to the tatwic calls of life. When we reach the animal kingdom the external tatwic foci are just visible. These are the sensuous organs, each of which has the capability of focusing its own peculiar tatwic rays into itself. In the lowest forms of animal life they are just visible, and this is a sign that the mental principle is then in a comparatively high state of perfection: it has begun to respond somewhat to the external tatwic call. It might be remarked here that this is the superposed relative mind, and not the absolute original mental truti, both of which I have already described. It is the uprising of this evolutionary finite structure on all the planes of life that has led a German philosopher to the conclusion that God is Becoming. This is true of course, but it is only true of the finite Universe of names and forms and not of the absolute towards which it is moving.

To resume: The exposure of this animal life to the external tatwas is longer and longer, and the strength becomes greater and greater in their various foci, the formation of these foci becomes higher and higher, the external call upon the mind is stronger and stronger, and the mental response is more and more perfect. A time comes in the progress of this mental evolution when the five mental senses are perfectly developed, as is marked by the development of the external senses. We call the action of the five mental senses the phenomenon of perception. On the manifesta-tion of this perception is raised the mighty fabric of perception of those mental manifestations that I have discussed in the essay on Mind. The way in which this evolution takes place is sketched there too.

The external tatwas of gross matter create gross foci in a gross body from whence to send their currents. The soul does the same. The tatwic currents of the external soul, Iswara, create similar centers of action in connection with the mind. But the tatwic vibrations of the soul are finer than those of the life-principle. The mental matter takes a longer time to respond to the call of Iswara than it does to answer to the call of Prana. It is not till the life- wave reaches humanity that the vibrations of the soul begin to show themselves in the mind. The foci of psychic currents are located in what is called the vijnana maya kosha, the psychic coil. At the time of the beginning of human life, the psychic foci go on gaining strength, race after race, till we reach the point that I have called the awakening of the soul. That process ends in the confirmation of the state of paravairagya. From this state there are only a few steps to the power of what has been called ulterior or psychic perception.

Our former perception may now be called animal perception. And just as the mighty fabric of inference and verbal authority has been raised on the basis of animal perception, a more mighty fabric of inference and verbal authority has been raised on the basis of psychic perception by ancient Aryan sages. We shall come to that by and bye.

As practice confirms the state of paravairagya in the Yogi's mind, it gets the most perfect calm. It is open to all sorts of tatwic influences, without any sensuous disturbance. The next power that consequently shows itself is called samapatti. I define this word as that mental state in which it becomes capable of receiving the reflection of the subjective and the objective worlds, and the means of knowledge at the slightest motion, however imparted.

Intuition has four stages: (1) Sa vitarka, verbal, (2) Nir vitarka, wordless, (3) Sa vichara, meditative, (4) Nir vichara, ultra-meditative.

The state of intuition has been likened to a bright, pure, transparent, colorless crystal. Place whatever you will behind such a crystal, and it will show itself in the color of that object. And so does the mind behave in this state. Let the tatwic rays that constitute the objective world fall on it, and it shows itself in the colors of the objective world. Remove these colors, and it is again as pure as crystal, ready to show in itself any other colors that might be presented to it. Think of the elementary forces of Nature, the tatwa, think of the gross objects where they work, think of the organs of sense and their genesis and the method of their operations, think of the soul, liberated or bound, and the mind readily falls into each of these states. It retains no particular color that might oppose or vitiate any other color entering it. The first stage of intuition is verbal. It is the most common in this age and therefore the most easily intelligible.

Let the reader think of a mind in which no color is evoked at the sound of scientific words. Let him think of thousands of those men in whose minds the sounds of their own language, full of high and great ideas, is as strange as Hebrew. Take an uneducated English peasant and teach him to read Comus. Do you think those beautiful words will carry to him all they are intended to convey? But why an uneducated peasant? Did the great Johnson himself understand the beauties of Milton? Take again a common schoolboy, and read to him in his own language the truths of philosophy. Does that language, even if you gave him its lexicographic meaning, convey any idea to his mind? Take the Upanishad, and read it to any pandit who can understand Sanskrit reasonably well. Does anyone doubt (I do not) that he does not understand all that those noble words convey? With such a mind, let him compare the mind of a really educated man, a mind that almost intuitively takes in the true sense of words. To take in the full sense that words are intended to convey is not an easy task, even for the highly educated. Prejudice, deep-seated antagonistic theories, the strength of one's own convictions, and perhaps some other characteristics of the mind prove to be an insurmountable obstacle. Even a John Stuart Mill could not properly understand the philosophy of Sir William Hamilton. One of the greatest Oriental scholars says that Patanjali's system is no philosophy at all! Another has expressed himself to the effect that Patanjali's Aphorisms on Yoga are mere fanaticism! There are many tantras of which, though we might translate them into any language, very few of us really know the meaning. This is a very grave shortcoming, and sometimes much to be regretted. It disappears only with the manifestation of verbal intuition. In this state the Yogi is at once en rapport with the author of the book, and this is because his mind is free from every blinding prejudice, and is in fact a pure, bright, colorless crystal, ready to show any phase of color that might come in contact with it.

The next stage of intuition is wordless. In this you no longer stand in need of books to initiate yourself into the secrets of nature. Your mind becomes capable of serving these truths from their fountainhead: true pictures of everything in every state of the objective word which through the agency of prana are represented in the universal mind, pictures that are the souls of these things, their own true selves, pregnant with every state in which the thing has passed, or has to pass, the realities of the various and varying phases of the phenomenal world, the thing which in a table, a glass, a pen, and in fact any and every thing, is hard or soft, long or short, white or black.

These state have for their object the gross phenomenal world. The next two stages of intuition have for their object the world of forces that lies at the root of the changes of the gross world, the world of subtle bodies. The meditative intuition has for its object only the present manifestation of the currents of the subtle body, the forces that are already showing or going to show themselves. In this state, for example, the Yogi knows intuitively the present forces of the atmospheric Prana as they are gathering strength enough to give us a shower of rain or snow, but he does not know what has given them their present activity, or whether the potential will ever become the actual, and if yes, to what extent. He knows the forces that are working at the present moment in that tree, that horse, that man, the powers that keep these things in the state they are in, but he does not know the antecedents and consequents of that state.

The next state has for its object all the three states of subtle bodies. The present state is know of course, but with it the Yogi draws in the whole history of the object from beginning to end. Place before him a rose, and he knows its subtle principle in all this states, antecedents and consequents. He is familiar with the little beginnings of the bush and its growth in various stages; he knows how the budding began, how the bud opened, and how it grows into a beautiful flower. He knows what its end shall be, and when. Put before him a closed letter, and he knows not only what that letter contains, but he can trace those thoughts to the brain whence they proceeded, to the hand that wrote the letter, to the room in which they were written, and so on. It is in this state too that the mind knows mind, without the medium of words.

These four states constitute what is called the objective trance (savija samadhi).

Occasionally these powers show themselves in many minds. But that simply shows that the favored mortal is on the right track. He must make sure of the point if he would win.

When the last stage of this samadhi is confirmed in the mind, our psychic senses gain the power of that amount of certain knowledge which is the portion of our animal senses. The authority of these senses is supreme with us, so far as the gross world is concerned. In a similar way there is no room left for us to doubt the truth of the knowledge that our psychic senses bring us. The high power of knowing every supersensuous truth with perfect certainty is known as Ritambhara, or psychic perception.

The knowledge that psychic perception gives us is by no means to be confounded with the knowledge obtained through inference, imagination, or the records of others' experience.

Inference, imagination, and verbal authority, based on animal perception, can only work upon knowledge obtained through animal senses. But psychic perception and inference based upon that has for its object things of the supersensuous world, the realities that underlie the phenomenal existence with which we are familiar. That perception takes in the fact of the existence and the nature of Prakriti, the most subtle state of matter, just as animal perception takes in gross matter.

Animal perception draws the mind towards gross matter, the world that has given it birth. So does psychic perception draw the mind towards the soul. The practice of objective samadhi destroys itself. The mind takes in so much of the higher energy of the soul that it loses its mental consistency. Down goes the entire structure of unreal names and forms. The soul lives in herself, and not in the mind as now.

With this the greater part of my work is done. It is now clear that what we call man lives chiefly in the mind. The mind has two entities to affect it. The one is the life-principle, the other the psychic principle, the once producing certain changes in the mind from below, the other from above. These changes have been recorded, and it has been found that the dominion of the soul is more desirable than that of the life principle. When the mind loses itself entirely in the soul, man becomes God.

The object of these essays has been roughly to portray the nature, function and mutual relation of the principles; in other words, to trace the operation of the universal tatwic law on all the planes of existence. This has been briefly done. A good deal more remains to be said about the powers latent in the Prana and the mind, which show themselves in special departments of the progress of man. That need not, however, form part of the present series, and therefore I close this series with some description of the first and last principle of the cosmos: the Spirit.

XV. The Spirit

This is the anandamaya kosha, literally the coil of bliss of the Vedantins. With the power of psychic perception, the soul knows the existence of this entity, but in the present stage of human development it has hardly made its presence directly felt in the human constitution. The characteristic difference between the soul and the spirit is the absence of the "I" in the latter.

It is the dawn of the day of evolution. It is the first setting-in of the positive current of the great breath. It is the first state of cosmic activity after the night of Mahapralaya. As we have seen, the breath in every state of existence has three states: the positive, the negative, and the susumna. The susumna is pregnant with either of the two states. This is the state that is described in the Parameshthi sukta of the Rig Veda as neither Sat (positive) nor Asat (negative). This is the primary state of parabrahma, in which the whole universe lies hidden like a tree in the seed. As billows rise and lose themselves in an ocean, the two states of evolution and involution take their rise in this state, and in due time are lost in the same. What is Prakriti itself in this state of potential omnipotence? The phenomena of Prakriti owe their origin and existence to the modifications of the great breath. When that great breath is in the state of susumna, can we not say that Prakriti itself is held in that state by susumna? It is in fact parabrahma that is all in all. Prakriti is only the shadow of that substance, and like a shadow it follows the modifications of His great breath. The first modification of the great breath is the setting in of the evolutionary (positive) current) In this state, Prakriti is ready to modify into the ethers of the first degree, which make up the atmosphere from which Iswara draws life. In the first state of evolution, the Subject (parabrahma) whose breath causes these modifications of Prakriti, is known as Sat, the fountainhead of all existence. The I is latent in this state. Naturally enough, because it is the differentiation that gives birth to the I. But what is this state? Must man be annihilated before he reaches this state of what from the standpoint of man is called nirvana or paranirvana? There is no reason to suppose that it is the state of annihilation any more than a certain amount of latent heat is annihilated in water. The simple fact is that the color that constitutes the ego becomes latent in the spirit's higher form of energy. It is a state of consciousness or knowledge above self, not certainly destroying it.

The individual spirit bears the same relation to the Sat which the individual soul bears to the Iswara, the individual mind to the Virat, and the individual life-principle to the Prana. Each center is given birth to by the tatwic rays of that degree. Each is a drop in its own ocean. The Upanishad explains this state under many names. The Chhandogva, however, has a very comprehensive dialogue on this subject between Uddalaka and his son Shwetakete.

Professor Max Muller has made some very questionable remarks on certain assertions in this dialogue, calling them "more or less fanciful". These remarks could never have fallen from so learned a man had he known and understood something of the ancient Science of Breath and the Philosophy of the Tatwas. The Upanishad can never be very intelligible without this comprehensive science. It must be remembered that the Upanishads themselves have in many places clearly laid down that a teacher is wanted for the proper understanding of these divine words. Now the teacher taught nothing else but the Science of Breath, which is said to be the secret doctrine of all secret doctrines. It is, in fact, the key to all that is taught in the Upanishad. The little book that tries to explain these essays to the world appears from its very arrangement to be a compilation of various couplets on the same subject, inherited from various esoteric circles. In fact, this handful of stanzas has its chief value as a key to Aryan philosophy and occult science, but even this little book will hardly serve to dispel the gloom of ages.

To return, however, to the dialogue between the father and the son: it is contained in the sixth Prapathaka of the Chhandogya Upanishad.

"In the beginning, my dear, there was only that which is one only, without a second. Others say in the beginning there was that only, which is not one only, without a second, and from which is not, that which is was born."

This is the translation of Professor max Muller. Notwithstanding the authority of his great name, and real scholarship, I venture to think that the sense of the Upanishad is totally lost sight of in this translation. The words of the original are:

"Sad eva saumyedamagre asit."

I cannot find any word in the translation giving the sense of the word idam in the original. Idam means "this", and it has been explained as meaning the phenomenal world. This that is perceived, etc. Therefore real translation of the text would be:

"This (world) was Sat alone in the beginning."

Perhaps in the translation of Professor Muller the word "there" is printed by mistake for "this". If this is the case, the defect in the translation is at once cured.

The text means that the first state of the world before differentiation was the state known as Sat. From what comes afterwards, it appears that this is the state of the Universe in which all its phenomena, material, mental and psychic, are held in posse. The word eva, which in the translation stands for the word "alone" or "only", signifies that in the beginning of the Day of Evolution the universe had not all the five, or even two or more of the five planes of existence together. Now such is the case, but in the beginning the Sat existed alone.

The Sat is one only, without a second. There is no qualification of time in these two epithets. The Sat is one alone, not like the Prana, the Virat, and Iswara, having all three existing simultaneously, a shadowy side of existence.

The next sentence goes on to say that in the beginning there was Asat alone. As Professor Muller renders it, "There [?] was that only which is not."

Now this carries no meaning, notwithstanding the Greek accompaniment. That the word Asat is used in the sense of "that which is not" or briefly "nothing", there is no doubt. But there is also no doubt that such is not the meaning of the Upanishad. The words are used here in the same sense in which they are used in the "Nosad asit" hymn of the Rigveda.

"Then there was neither the Sat nor the Asat."

This of course is a state quite other than the Sat of the Upanishad. It is nothing more than the susumna of the Brahmic breath. After this in the beginning of evolution the Brahma became Sat. This is the positive potential phase. The Asat is nothing more than the cooler negative life current that rules during the night of Maha pralaya. When the shadowy Prakriti has undergone the preparatory influence of the negative current, the day of evolution sets in with the beginning of the positive current. The dispute as to beginning is merely of a technical nature. In reality there is no beginning. It is all a motion in the circle, and from this point of view we may put whatever state we like in the beginning.

But the Asat philosopher argues that unless the Maya undergo the preparatory influence of the Night, there can be no creation. Hence, according to him, we must put Asat at the beginning.

The sage Uddalaka would not consent to this. According to him, the active impressive force is in the Sat, the positive state, just as all the life-forms take their origin from Prana (the positive life matter) and not from Rayi (the negative life matter) – see the Prasnopnishat. It is only impressibility that exists I the Asat; the real names and forms of the phenomenal Universe do not exist there. In fact, the name Asat has been given to the primary state of the evolving universe for this very reason. If we would translate these two words into English, we would have to coin two very unique compounds: Sat (that-in-which- is) and Asat (that-in-which-is-not).

It is only such a rendering that would carry the true idea, and hence it is advisable to retain the Sanskrit words and explain them as well as one can.

That actually existing state in which the names and forms do not exist cannot very properly stand as the cause of the names and forms that do not exist. Hence the Sat alone was in the beginning, etc.

The individual spirit has the same relation to the Sat as the soul has to the Iswara.

That will do for now. It is enough to show that there is no annihilation anywhere in the Universe. Nirvana simply means the enlightenment (which is not extinction) of the phenomenal rays.

The Science of Breath & The Philosophy of the

Tatwas

(Translated from the Sanskrit)

1. The goddess said: My Lord Mahadeva, the god of gods, be kind to me, and tell me the wisdom that comprehends everything.

2. How did the universe come out? How does it go on? How does it disappear? Tell me, O Lord, the philosophy of the universe.

===

Notes ~ "The god said"; "the goddess said"; "said the god"; "said the goddess". The whole book is couched in the form of a dialogue between the god Siva and his wife Parvati. All the tantras have the same form. It is hardly consistent with facts to hold that Siva and Parvati were a human pair in some ancient period. The former is generally spoken of in this book as Iswara, the latter as Devi or Shakti. Judging from its method of composition, the book under notice does not seem to have been written by Siva. In the first place, there are several stanzas in the book that appear to be the composition of different authors, but in the present form by some compiler. Secondly, the author says in one place that he was going to describe certain experiments as he had seen them in the Sivagama (The Teaching of Siva). In the end of one ms., however, it si said that the book comprises the eighth chapter of Sivagama.

In the Kenopnishat the great commentator Shankaracharya interprets Uma Haimvait (another name of Parvati) as Brahma Vidya, the Divine Science or Theosophia. There, however, the goddess appears as a teacher-ess, and she might well be interpreted as Theosophia. That explanation will hardly hold good here. Here Siva and Parvati seem to be the male and female principles. They are the best acquainted with their own workings.
The god, the male principle, explaining to Sakti, the female principle, the various modes in which the finer forces of nature imprint themselves upon the grosser planes, might be the symbol of the eternal impression of all thoughts and living organisms into the Sakti (the cooler matter rayi) by Siva, the hotter male principle.

3. Said the god: The universe came out of tatwa or the tatwas; it goes on by the instrumentality of the tatwas; it disappears in the tatwas; by the tatwas is known the nature of the universe.

Notes ~ In the original the singular number is often used to denote the common quality of the five tatwas, that by which each is known as such.

The universe comprehends all the manifestations with which we are familiar, either on the physical, the mental, or the psychic plane. All of them have come out of the tatwas. The tatwas are the forces that lie at the root of all these manifestations Creation, preservation, and destruction, or more strictly speaking, appearance, sustenance, and disappearance of the phenomena with which we are acquainted are tatwic changes of state.

4. Said the goddess: The Knowers of the tatwas have ascertained the tatwa to be the highest root; what, O God, is the nature of the tatwas? Throw light upon the tatwas.

5. Said the god: Unmanifested, formless, one giver of light is the great Power; from that appeared the soniferous ether (akasa); from that had birth the tangiferous ether.

Notes ~ This is the parabrahma of the Vedantins, the first change of state that stands at the top of evolution. This is the first positive phase of life. All the Upanishads concur in this. In the beginning all this was Sat (the positive phase of Brahma). From this state the five ethers (tatwas or mahabhutas as they are also called) come out by degrees. "From him came the Akasa and so on", said the Upanishad. This state of parabrahma is called in the text "Unmanifested". Manifestation for us only begins with the "Ego", the sixth principle of our constitution; all beyond that is naturally unmanifested, "Formless". This epithet is given because forms only show themselves when the tatwas and the two states of matter, the male and female, the hotter and the cooler, come into existence. As yet there is only one universal state of matter. Hence that state is also given the epithet One.

He is also called the Giver of Light. This light is the real life. It is this state that transmutes into the five ethers that form the atmosphere of the sixth principle of the universe.

6. From the tangiferous ether, the luminiferous ether, and from this the gustiferous ether; from thence was the birth of the odiferous ether. These are the five ethers and they have five-fold extension.

7. Of these the universe came out; by these it goes on; into these it disappears; even among these it shows itself again.

8. The body is made of the five tatwas; the five tatwas, O Fair One, exist therein in the subtle form; they are known by the learned who devote themselves to the tatwas.

Notes ~ The body, human as well as every other, is made of the five tatwas in their gross form. In this gross body play the five tatwas in their subtle form. They govern it physiologically, mentally, psychically and spiritually. These are therefore the four subtle forms of the tatwas.

9. On this account shall I speak of the rise of breath in the body; by knowing the nature of inspiration and expiration comes into being the knowledge of the three times.

Notes ~ Man can devote himself most easily to his own body. On this account the laws of the rise of the breath in the body have been described here.

Knowledge of the three times (the past, the present and the future) is nothing more than a scientific knowledge of the causes and effects of phenomena. Know the present tatwic state of things, know its antecedent and consequent states, and you have a knowledge of the three times.

10. This science of the rise of breath, the hidden of the hidden, the shower of the true Good, is a pearl on the head of the wise.

11. This knowledge is the subtle of the subtle; it is easily understood; it causes the belief of people.

12. The science of the rise of breath is to be given to the calm, the pure, the virtuous, the firm and the grateful, single-minded devote of the guru.

13. It is not to be given to the vicious, the impure, the angry, the untruthful, the adulterer, and him who has wasted his substance.

14. Hear, thou goddess, the wisdom which is found in the body; omniscience is caused by it, if well understood.

15. In the swara are the Vedas and the shastras; in the swara the highest gandharva; in the swara are all the three worlds; the swara is the reflection of the parabrahma.

Notes ~ "In the swara are the Vedas", etc. Swara is the current of the life-wave. It is the same as the intelligence of the Vedantins. The assertion in this stanza might have two meanings. It might mean that the things described in the Vedas are in the swara, or it might mean that the description itself is there. It might mean that both are there. This is of course an absolute fact. There is nothing in the manifested universe that has not received existence from the Great Breath, which is the Prana of the universe on the highest plane of life.

16. Without a knowledge of the breath (swara), the astrologer is a

hose without its lord, a speaker without learning, a trunk without a head.

17. Whoever knows the analysis of the Nadis, and the Prana, the analysis of the tatwa, and the analysis of the conjunctive susumna gets salvation.

18. It is always auspicious in the seen or the unseen universe, when the power of breath is mastered; they, O Fair One, that the knowledge of the science of breath is somewhat auspicious.

Notes ~ This stanza points to the difference between practical and theoretical occultism. The practice is highly auspicious, of course, but the theory too puts us on the right track, and therefore is somewhat auspicious.

19. The parts and the first accumulations of the universe were made by the swara, and the swara is visible as the great Power, the Creator, and the Destroyer.

Notes ~ For some reflections on this subject, the reader is referred to the Essay on Evolution.

20. A knowledge more secret than the science of Breath, wealth more useful than the science of Breath, a friend more true than the science of breath, was never seen or heard of.

21. An enemy is killed during the power of the breath, and also friends are brought together; wealth is got during the power of breath, and comfort and reputation during the same.

Notes ~ Every phenomenon is nothing more than a phase of tatwic motion.

22. On account of the force of breath one gets a female child or meets a king; by the force of breath are gods propitiated, and by the breath is a king in anyone's power.

23. Locomotion is caused by the power of breath, and food too is taken by the power of breath; urine and faeces also are discharged during the power of breath.

24. All the Sastras and Purana, etc., beginning with the Vedas and the Upanishads, contain no principle beyond the knowledge of swara (the breath).

25. All are names and forms. Among all these people wander mis-

taken. They are fools steeped in ignorance unless the tatwas are known.

Notes ~ All the phenomena f the universe are names and forms. All these names and forms is distinguishable. They are only distinguished as such when they are imprinted upon the grosser planes. The impression takes place by the instrumentality of Rayi, the cooler state of life-matter, which is only the shade of Prana, the original state. Hence the names and forms are all unreal.

26. This science of the rise of breath is the highest of all the high sciences; it is a flame for illuminating the mansion of the soul.

27. The knowledge cannot be imparted to this man or that man except in answer to a question; it is therefore to be known by one's own exertions in the soul, by the soul, and soul alone.

Notes ~ This is the celebrated dictum, "Know thyself by thyself", which differs from the Greek one in the addition of the last two words.

28. Neither the lunar day, nor the constellations, nor the solar day, nor planet, nor god; neither rain nor the Vyatipata, nor the conjunctions Vaidhrita, etc.

Notes ~ These are all of them the various phases of the five different tatwic states. They have a natural effect upon the terrestrial life. The effect differs with the thing influenced. The rays of the tatwic state of time will only be reflected into any organism if the reflecting surface is akin. The yogi who has power over his breath can put it into any tatwic state he chooses, and the antagonistic effect of time are simply thrown off.

29. Nor the bad conjunctions, goddess, ever have power; when one gets the pure power of swara, everything has good effect.

30. In the body are the Nadi having many forms and well extended; they ought to be known in the body by the wise, for the sake of knowledge.

31. Branching off from the root in the navel, 72,000 of them extend in the body.

Notes ~ The Yogi takes the navel to be the starting point of the system of Nadi. So says Patanjali, the great Yogi philosopher:

"The systems of the body are known by concentration on the navel."

The Vedantins take the heart to be the starting point of the system. The former assign as the reason, the existence in the navel of the Power Kundalini, the latter the existence in the heart of the cardiac soul (the Lingam atma), which is the real life of the gross body. This, however, is immaterial. We may begin wherever we like, if we only understand truly the location of the life-principle and its various manifestations.

32. In the navel is the Power Kundalini sleeping like a serpent; thence ten Nadi go upwards and ten downwards.

Notes ~ "The Power Kundalini": This power sleeps in the developed organism. It is that power which draws in gross matter from the mother organism through the umbilical cord, and distributes it to the different places where the seminal Prana gives it form. When the child separates from the mother the Power goes to sleep. She is no more wanted now. The dimensions of the child depend upon the supplies of the Kundalini. It is said that it is possible to awake the goddess even in the undeveloped organism by certain practices of Yoga. When this is done the Yogi gets the power of lengthening or shortening the limbs.

33. Two and two of the Nadi go crosswise; they are thus twenty-four in number. The principal are the ten Nadi in which act the ten forces.

34. Crosswise, or upwards, or downwards, in them is manifested the prana all over the body. They are in the body in the shape of Chakras supporting all the manifestations of Prana.

35. Of all these, ten are principal; out of the ten, three are the highest: Ida, Pingala, and the Susumna.

36. Gandhari, Hastijihva, Pusha and Yashaswani; Alambusha, Kuhui, Sankhini, and also Damini.

37. Ida is in the left part, Pingala in the right, Susumna in the middle; Gandhari in the left eye.

38. In the right eye Hastijihva; in the right ear Pusha; Yashaswani in the left ear; in the mouth Alambusha.

39. Kuhu in the place of the generative organ; in the anus Shankhini. In this way one at each outlet stand the Nadi.

40. Ida, Pingala, and Susumna stand in the way of the Prana, these ten Nadi extend variously in the body.

Notes ~ For a dissertation on these three Nadi, the reader is referred to the articles on Prana. On a small scale, the right and left chambers of the heart and the right and left portions of the spinal column are the Pingala and Ida. The canal between these two is the Susumna. Taking the blood vessel system to be a mere reflection of the nervous system, the terminology might be applied to the nervous alone. It appears, however, that the Nadi of the Tantra comprehend both these systems. In the nervous system there is the real power, and this must be present everywhere where there is any manifestation of life.

41. These are the names of the Nadis. Now I give the names of the forces: (1) Prana, (2) Apana, (3) Samana, (4) Udana, and (5) Vyana .

42. (6) Naga, (7) Kurma, (8) Krikila, (9) Devadatta, and (10) Dhananjaya. In the chest lives always the prana; the apana in the circle of the anus.

43. The Samana in the circle of the navel, the Udana in the midst of the throat; the Vyana pervades all over the body. These are the ten principal forces.

44. The five beginning with the Prana have been described. The remaining five begin with
Naga. Their names and places too I give:

45. The Naga is known in belching; the Kurma in the twinkling of the eye; the Krikila is known as the cause of hunger; the Devadatta is known in yawning.

46. The all-pervading Dhananjaya does not leave even the dead body. All these move in all the Nadis where they put on the appearance of life.

47. Let the wise man know the manifest movements of the individualized prana by the three Nadi: Ida, Pingala, and Susumna.

48. The Ida is to be known in the left half and the Pingala in the right.

49. The moon is placed in the Ida; the sun in the Pingala; the Susumna has the nature of Sambhu, and Sambhu is the self of Hansa [inspiration and expiration both].

50. Expiration is called Ha; inspiration is Sa; Ha is the Siva [the male], and Sa the Sakti [the female].

51. Appearing as Sakti, stands the moon, causing the left Nadi to flow; causing the right Nadi to flow, the sun appears as Sambhu [male].

52. Any charity given by the wise while the breath is in the left nostril, multiplies krore upon krore of times in this world.

53. Let the Yogi look into his face, with one mind and with attention, and thus let him know entirely the motion of the sun and the moon.

54. Let him meditate upon the tatwa when the prana is calm, never when it is disturbed; his desire will be fulfilled, he will have great benefit and victory.

55. To those men who practice, and thus always keep the sun and moon in proper order, knowledge of the past and the future becomes as easy as if they were in their hand.

56. In the left Nadi the appearance of the breath is that of the Amrita (Nectar); it is the great nourisher of the world. In the right, the motion-imparting portion, the world is always born.

Notes ~ A krore = 10 million. The Negative phase of Prana has the qualities of Amrita, the giver of eternal life. The negative matter, the moon, is cooler than the positive matter, the sun. The former is Rayi, the latter Prana. The former receives the impressions from the latter, and this plays the part of imparting impressions to that. The moon, therefore, is the real life of all names and forms. In her they live; she keeps them up. She is, therefore, the Amrita, the nectar of life. The right Nadi is, from the greater temperature it possesses, the imparter of names and forms, or briefly, the motion-imparting phase of life matter. It is the tendency of the sun to always cause changes in names and forms, and giving new impressions in the place of the old. Hence the sun is the great destroyer of forms. He is the father of the forms, but the real preserver is the moon.

57. The middle one, the susumna, moves very cruelly, and is very bad in all acts; everywhere in auspicious acts the left [Nadi] causes strength.

58. In going out the left is auspicious; in going in the right is auspicious; the moon must be known to be even, the sun odd.

59. The moon is female, the sun is male; the moon is fair, the sun is dark [as compared to the moon]. During the flow of the Nadi of the moon let calm acts be done.

60. During the flow of the Nadi of the sun harsh works are to be done; during the flow of the susumna are to be done acts resulting in the attainments of psychic powers and salvation.

61. In the bright fortnight the moon comes in first, in the dark one the sun; beginning from the first lunar day they rise one after the other in order, after three days each.

62. The moon and the sun have each the white [northward, upward]

and the black [southward, downward] duration of 2-1/2 ghari. They flow in order during the 60 ghari of a day.

63. Then by a ghari each [24 minutes] the five tatwas flow. The days begin with the pratipat [the first lunar day]. When the order is reversed the effect is reversed.

64. In the bright fortnight the left [is powerful], in the dark the right; let the yogi with attention bring these into order, beginning with the first lunar day.

65. If the breath rises [at sunrise] by way of the moon, and sets in by that of the sun, it confers groups of good qualities; in the reverse, the reverse.

66. Let the moon flow the whole day through, and the sun the whole night; he who practices thus is no doubt a yogi.

67. The moon is checked by the sun, the sun by the moon; he who knows this practice, tramples in a moment over the three worlds.

68. During Thursdays, Fridays, Wednesdays and Mondays the left Nadi gives success in all acts, especially in the white fortnight.

69. During Sundays, Tuesdays and Saturdays the right Nadi gives success in all harsh acts, especially in the black fortnight.

70. During the five gharis each, the tatwas have their distinct rise in order, ghari by ghari.

71. Thus there are twelve changes during the day and night. The Taurus, Cancer, Virgo, Scorpio, Capricorn, and Pisces are in the moon [i.e., the breath rises in the left Nadi in these signs].

72. During Aries, Gemini, Leo, Libra, Sagittarius, and Aquarius the rise of the breath is in the right Nadi. From this good or bad is ascertained.

73. The sun is centered in the east and north, the moon in the west and south. Let none go west and south during the flow of the right Nadi.

74. Let none go east and north during the flow of the left Nadi; if anyone does go, he will have the fear of robbers and will not return.

75. The wise who desire good might not therefore go in these directions during these intervals; then there doubtlessly will be suffering and death.

76. When the moon flows during the bright fortnight, it is beneficial to the man; comfort is caused in mild deeds.

77. When the moon rises at the time of the rise of breath, and vice versa, quarrel and danger make appearance, and all good disappears.

The Wrong Swara ~

78. When in the morning the wrong breath takes its rise, that is the sun in place of the moon, and the moon in place of the sun, then:

79. During the first day the mind is confused; during the second loss of wealth; during the third they speak of motion; during the fourth the destruction of the desired [object].

80. During the fifth the destruction of worldly position; during the sixth the destruction of all objects; during the seventh disease and pain; during the eight, death.

81. When for these eight days, at all the three times, the breath is wrong, then the effect is simply bad. When there is something less there is some good.

82. When in the morning and the noon there is the moon, and in the evening the sun, then there is always success and benefit. The reverse gives pain.

83. Whenever the breath is in the right or the left Nadi, the journey will be successful if the right or the left, as the case may be, is the first step.

84. Going four steps [by the left step first] when the moon flows, and five steps [by the right step first] when the sun flows, causes success all over the three worlds.

85. One must go on an even number of steps during the moon, and an odd one during the sun, raising first the foot [belong to the] full Nadi.

86. If by the hand of that part of the body in which the breath might be flowing at the time of waking, one touches his face, he is successful in his desires.

87. In taking a thing from another, and in going out of the house, we take by the hand in whose corresponding half the Nadi flows, and begin motion by raising the same foot.

88. There will be no confusion, no quarrel, no piercing with thorns; he will come back comfortable and free from all accidents.

89. Those who desire success in their undertakings must talk with teachers, relations, kings, and ministers and others who can fulfill one's desires, keeping them towards the full half of the body.

90. Those who desire success, benefit, and comfort must talk with enemies, thieves, creditors, and such others, keeping them towards the empty half of the body.

91. To distant countries one must go during the moon; to rather near countries during the sun.

92. Whatever of income, etc., and comings together, has been described before, comes to pass without doubt in the Nadis notices before.

93. Whatever has been said before to be the effect of the empty Nadi, is all in accordance with what has been said by the omniscient.

94. All transactions or dealings with bad men where there is enmity or deceit, angry lords or thieves, etc., are dangerous towards the full half of the body.

95. In going on a distant journey, the moon is auspicious, and gives ceaseless success in the aim; the sun is good in coming in, and in the beginning of any hasty work.

96. During the flow of the moon, poison is destroyed; during that of the sun, power is obtained over any body. During the susumna salvation is obtained. One power stands in three forms: the sun, the moon, and the susumna.

97. It might happen that when something is to be done, the breath is not rightly flowing, or conversely, when the breath is flowing as it ought to be, there is no occasion for the action to be done. How then is a man of business to follow the promptings of prana?

98. Auspicious or inauspicious acts are always to be done day and night. When need be the proper Nadi is to be set in motion.

The Ida ~

99. In those acts which are desired to have durable effect, in going on a distant journey, in entering an order of life (Ashrama) or a palace, in amassing wealth;

100. In sinking wells, ponds, tanks, etc, in erecting columns and idols, in buying utensils, in marriage, in having clothes, jewels and ornaments prepared;

101. In preparing cooling and nourishing divine medicines, in seeing one's lord, in trade, in collection of grain;

102. In going into a new house, in taking charge of some office, in cultivation, in throwing the seed, in auspicious peace-making, in going out, the moon is auspicious.

103. In such acts as beginning to read, etc., in seeing relations... in virtue, in learning from some spiritual teacher, in rehearsing a Mantra;

104. In reading the aphorisms of the Science of Time, in bringing quadrupeds home, in the treatment of diseases, in calling upon masters;

105. In riding horses and elephants, in doing good to others, in making deposits;

106. In singing, in playing upon instruments, in thinking of the science of musical sounds, in entering any town, in coronation;

107. In disease, sorrow, dejection, fever, and swoon, in establishing relations with one's people, in entering any town or village, in coronation;

108. In the adornment of their person by women, when the rain is coming, in the worship of the teacher, in preparing poisons, etc., O Fair One! The moon is auspicious.

109. Also such acts as the practice of Yoga give success in Ida. Even in Ida let one give up the akasa and taijas modifications of prana.

110. In day or in night all works are successful; in all auspicious works the flow of the moon is good.

The Pingala ~

111. In all harsh acts, in the reading and teaching of difficult sciences... in getting into a ship;

112. In all bad acts, in drinking, in rehearsing the Mantra of such a god as Bhairava, in administering poison to enemies;

113. In learning the Shastras, in going, in hunting, in the selling of animals, in the difficult collection of bricks, wood, stone and jewels, etc.;

114. In the practice of music, in the Yantras and tantras, in climbing a high place or mountain, in gambling, in theft, in the breaking of an elephant or a horse, in a carriage or otherwise.

115. In riding a new donkey, camel, or buffalo, or an elephant or horse, in crossing a stream, in medicine, in writing;

116. In athletic sports, in killing or producing confusion, in practicing the six Karmas, etc., in obtaining power of Yakshinis, Yakshas, Vetalas, Poisons and Bhutas, etc.;

117. In killing, in causing love… in enmity, in mesmerizing, causing one to do anything at bidding, in drawing anyone towards anything, in causing distress and confusion, in charity, and buying and selling.

118. In practicing with swords, in inimical battle, in amorous enjoyment, in seeking the king, in eating, in bathing, in mercantile negotiations, in harsh and hot deeds, the sun is auspicious.

119. Just after eating… in winning the favor of women, the sun is auspicious. The wise ought to sleep, too, during the flow of the sun breath.

120. All harsh acts, all those various acts which in their nature must be transitory and temporary, find success during the sun. There is no doubt in this.

The Susumna ~

121. When the breath moves one moment in the left and the other in the right, the [state of prana] too is known a susumna. It is the destroyer of acts.

Notes ~ It will be seen that in this section three phases of the Susumna have been noticed: (1) When the breath comes one moment out of one nostril and next out of the other; (2) When the breath at once flows out of both nostrils with equal force; (3) When the breath flows out of one nostril with greater force than it does out of the other. The first is called the Unequal state (Vishamabhava). The second and third are called the Vishuvat or Vishuva.

122. When the prana is in that Nadi the fires of death burn. It is called Vishuvat, the destroyer of all actions.

123. When both the Nadis, which ought to flow one after the other, then without doubt there is danger for him who is thus afflicted.

124. When it is at one moment in the right, the other moment in the left, it is called the unequal state. The effect is the reverse of what is desired, and so it ought to be known, O Fair One!

125. The wise call it Vishuvat when both the Nadis flow. Do neither harsh not mild acts at that time; both will be fruitless.

126. In life, in death, in asking questions, in income, or its absence, in success or its want, everywhere the reverse is the case during the flow of the Vishuvat. Remember then the Lord of the Universe.

127. The Iswara is to be remembered by acts such as the practice of Yoga; nothing else is to be done at that time by those who desire success, income and comfort.

128. Pronounce a curse or benediction when with the sun the Susumna flows slowly; it will all be useless.

129. When the unequal state takes rise, do not so much as think of journeying. Journeying during this state undoubtedly causes pain and death.

130. When the Nadi changes or the tatwa changes, nothing auspicious shall be done by way of charity, etc.

131. In the front, in the left, and above is the moon. On the back, on the right, and below is the sun. in this way the wise ought to know the distinction between the full and empty.

Notes ~ Two or more phases of conjunction have been noticed: (1) Sandhya Sandhi, and (2) Vedoveda.

According to some philosophers, these do not exist. These two are said to be but the names of the two foregoing ones. This, however, is not the thesis of the present writer. He holds that both these states exist separately.

The Sandhya Sandhi is that Susumna through which disappearance takes place into the higher matter beyond. The physiological Susumna is the reservoir of man's potential physiological life. From that state takes its birth either the positive or the negative phase of life.

But the Susumna is the child of a higher phase of life. The positive and negative mental forces according to similar laws give birth to this

potential pranamaya kosha. The world, as some writers have said, is the
outcome of mental motion (Sankala, Meinah sphurana). The state of the
conjunction of these two mental states is the Sandhya Sandhi. The same
name seems to have been given to the higher susumna. When the two
phases of mental matter are neutralized in the Susumna, the pranamaya
kosha loses its vitality and disappears.

This is that state in which is thrown the reflection of the Higher Atma,
and from whence it is possible for it to come into the mind.

132. The Messenger who is above, in front, or on the left, is in the
way of the moon, and he who is below in the back and on the front, is in
the way of the sun.

133. The conjunction, which has no beginning, is One, and is without
[potential] nourishment or confusion – that through which disappearance takes place in the subtle matter beyond – is called Sandhya Sandhi.

134. Some say there is no separate Sandhya Sandhi, but the state in
which the prana is in the Vishuvat is called Sandhya Sandhi.

135. There is no separate Vedoveda; it does not exist. That conjunction
is called Vedoveda by which the highest Atma is known.

The Tatwas ~

136. Said the goddess: Great Lord! God of the gods! In thy mind is
the great secret that gives salvation to the world; tell me all that.

137. Said the god: There is no God beyond the secret knowledge of
breath; the Yogi who is devoted to the science of breath is the highest Yogi.

138. Creation takes place from the five tatwas; the tatwa disappears
in tatwa; the five tatwas constitute the objects of the highest knowledge;
beyond the five tatwas is the Formless.

139. The Prithivi, the Apas, the Taijas, the Vayu, and the Akasa are the
five tatwas; everything is of the five tatwas. Revered is he who knows this.

140. In the beings of all the worlds the tatwas are the same all over;
from the Satyaloka the arrangement of Nadi only differs.

Notes ~ See the Essay on the Tatwas. How everything, every possible
phenomenon of the soul, the mind, the prana, and the gross matter is of
the tatwas, the introductory Essays have tried to explain.

The nervous system is different in all the lokas. It has been said many a time that the tatwic rays flying in every direction from every point give birth to innumerable truti that are minimized pictures of the macrocosm. Now it will be easy to understand that these pictures are formed in different planes, which are differently inclined to the solar axis, and lie at different distances from the sun. Our planet is at a certain distance from the sun, and life is so arranged on this planet that the lunar and solar life-currents must have equal force if the organism is to be maintained. The tatwas also must be balanced. There might be other planes of life in which the respective powers of the two currents and the tatwas might be greater or less than they are on the earth. This difference will secure a difference in the arrangements of the Nadi, and also in their shape.

We experience this sort of thing even on our earth. Different animals and vegetables have different shapes. This is simply on account of the different truti stretching on different planes, differently inclined to the solar axis. Suppose for the sale of illustration that the following is the sphere of the macrocosmic prana:

Works on astrology assign different organs to these astral divisions, and for the purpose of illustration I shall assume these without further explanation. Thus we have on a larger scale:

These twelve regions comprehend the whole body in and out. Now suppose that there is a plane A-B having a certain inclination to the axis of the sun, S. From every point in the twelve regions rays fall in every truti of the plane A-B. Then there are other planes, C-D and E-F, etc.

It is evident that the rays falling on all these planes from the twelve regions will vary in relative strength and position on different planes. It is evident that on all these planes the different organs will differ in shape, in strength, and in relative position. This gives birth to more or less varying nervous systems in all the lokas, and the various shapes of the organisms of the earth.

As in evolution the necessities of the mind are changed, the pranamaya Koshas change their planes, and it is thus that they are changed on earth according to the occult theory of evolution.

141. In the left as well as the right there is the five-fold rise [of the tatwas]. The knowledge of the tatwas is eight-fold. Hear me, O Fair One: I shall tell thee.

142. The first is the number of the tatwas; the second the conjunction of breath; the third are the signs of the breath; the fourth the place of the tatwas;

143. The fifth is the color of the tatwas; the sixth is the prana itself; the seventh is their taste; the eighth is their mode of vibration.

144. Hear of the three-fold Prana: the Vishuvata, the Active [chara, the motor, sun], the Passive [achara or sthira, the receiver of motion, the moon] – in these eight forms. There is nothing, O Lotus-Faced Goddess, beyond the breath.

145. When by the effect of time the power of seeing does come it must be seen with great effort. The Yogi acts for the purpose of deceiving time.

Notes ~ "The Yogi acts for the purpose of deceiving time." Time is the order of appearance of the various tatwic phases of a living organism. In man this order is regulated by his previous Karma. By the power of previous Karma, the human organism assumes different receptive states, and in accordance with the receptivity the tatwic influence of time – the solar prana – cause pains or enjoyments of different sorts.

By the practice of Yoga the Yogi masters the tatwic changes of his body. Time is cheated. If he pushes the germ of disease out of his body no epidemic will ever affect him.

146. Let a man shut his ears by his thumbs, his nostrils by the middle fingers, his mouth by the last fingers and those last but one, and his eyes by the remaining fingers.

147. In this state the five tatwas are gradually known as the yellow, the white, the red, the blue, and the spotted without any other distinct upadhi [differentia].

148. Looking into a mirror, let the breath be thrown upon it; thus let the wise man know the difference among the tatwas by their forms.

149. Quadrangular, semi-lunar, triangular, spherical, and spotted are respectively the forms of the five tatwas.

150. Thus the first, prithivi, flows midway; the second, apas, flows downward; the third, agni, flows upwards; the fourth, vayu, flows at acute angles; the akasa flows between every two.

151. The apas tatwa is white; the prithivi yellow; the agni red; the vayu sky-blue; the akasa foreshadows every color.

152. First of all flows the vayu tatwa; secondly, the taijas; thirdly, the prithivi; and fourthly, the apas.

153. Between the two shoulders is located agni; in the root of the navel vayu; in the knees the apas; in the feet the prithivi; in the head the akasa.

154. The prithivi tatwa is sweet; the apas astringent; the taijas pungent; the vayu acid; the akasa bitter.

155. The vayu flows eight fingers breadth; the agni four; the prithivi twelve; the apas sixteen.

156. The upward motion tends to death; the downward to calmness; the one at acute angles to restlessness; the middle one to endurance; the akasa is common to all.

157. During the flow of the prithivi are performed acts which are expected to live long; during the apas passive acts; during the taijas harsh acts; during the vayu, killing, etc.

158. Nothing ought to be done during the akasa except the practice of Yoga; all other acts will remain without their desired effect.

159. During the prithivi and the apas success is obtained ; death comes in the taijas; reduction in the vayu. The akasa is known by the tatwic philosophers to be altogether useless.

160. During the prithivi income is late; during the apas, immediate; loss comes into existence by the taijas and the vayu; akasa is altogether useless.

161. The prithivi tatwa is yellow, has slow motion, moves in the middle, comes in its flow up to the end of the sternum, is heavy in sound, has slight heat in temperature. It gives success in works that are expected to stay long.

162. The apas tatwa is white, has rapid motion, moves downwards, comes in its flow sixteen fingers downward [up to the navel], is heavy in sound, is cool in temperature.

163. The taijas tatwa is red, moves in whirls [avartagah], moves upwards, comes in its flow four fingers downwards [up to the end of the chin], is very high in temperature. It gives birth to harsh actions [actions which, so to speak, set one on fire].

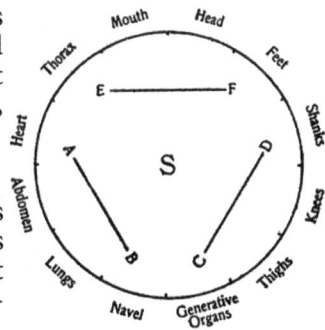

164. The vayu tatwa is sky-blue, moves at acute angles, comes in flow eight fingers downward, is hot or cool in temperature. It gives success in those works that are transitory.

165. The akasa tatwa is the common surface of all, foreshadows the qualities of all the tatwas. It gives yoga to the yogi.

166. Yellow and quadrangular, sweet and moving in the middle, and the giver of enjoyment is the prithivi tatwa, which flows twelve fingers downwards.

167. White, semi-lunar, astringent, moving downwards, and the causer of benefit is the apas tatwa, which is sixteen fingers in flow.

168. ---

169. Blue, spherical, acid, moving at acute angles, the giver of loco-motion is the vayu tatwa, which is eight fingers in flow.

170. Foreshadowing all colors, of the shape of an ear, bitter in taste, moving everywhere through the giver of Moksha is the akasa tatwa, which is useless in all worldly works.

171. The prithivi and the apas are auspicious tatwas, the taijas is middling in its effects, the akasa and vayu are inauspicious and cause loss and death to mankind.

172. The apas tatwa is in the east; the prithivi in the west; the vayu in the north; the taijas in the south; the akasa in the middle corners.

173. When the prithivi and the apas are in the moon, and the agni in the sun, then there is doubtless success in mild and harsh acts respectively.

174. The prithivi causes income during the day, the apas during the night; death comes in the taijas; reduction in the vayu; the akasa some-times burns.

175. In fitness for living, in success, in income, in cultivation [or: in enjoyment and growth], in amassing wealth, in understanding the meaning of the mantras, in questions about battle, in coming and going;

176. Benefit results during the apas tatwa; auspicious stay wherever it is during the prithivi; by the vayu they go away elsewhere; the akasa and the taijas cause loss and death.

177. In the prithivi comes the thought of roots [Mala]; in the apas and the vayu that of living things; in the taijas comes the thought of minerals; in the akasa there is void.

178. In the prithivi one thinks of beings of many feet; in the apas and vayu of bipeds; in the taijas of quadrupeds; in the akasa of the footless.

179. Mars is said to be the taijas, the Sun the prithivi, Saturn the apas,

and the Rahu the
vayu in the right Nadi.

180. The Moon is in the apas, Jupiter the prithivi, Mercury the vayu, and Venus the taijas in the left Nadi; for all acts doubtless.

Notes ~ The tatwic value of the planets described in these two verses seems to be the opinion of only a few. The opinion of the writer, which is also the opinion of the great astrologer Varahamchira, is expressed in stanza 181.

181. Jupiter is the prithivi; the Moon and Venus are the apas; the Sun and Mars are the taijas; the Dragon, the Ketu, and Saturn are Vayu; Mercury is the akasa.

182. Say during the prithivi the question that is about earthly things [roots, mala]; during the apas about life; during the taijas about minerals; during the akasa nothing.

183. Leaving the Sun and the Moon, when the breath goes to the Rahu know that it [prana] is in motion and desires another place.

184. (1) Pleasure, 92) growth, (3) affection, (4) playfulness, (5) success, (6) laughing, (7) in the prithivi and the apas; want of power in the organs, (8) fever, (9) trembling, (10) going out of one's country in the taijas and vayu.

185. (11) Loss of the life, substance, (12) and death in the akasa – these twelve are the phases of the moon [i.e., the forms, etc., that the negative matter assumes]; they ought always to be known with pains by the wise.

Notes ~ These twelve are the phases of the moon. The moon here means the power that gives sustenance to names and forms. That power, the rayi, appears in twelve forms, according to tatwic changes. The flow of the left Nadi in its diurnal course is not meant here.

186. In the East, the West, the South, and the North, the tatwas, prithivi, etc., are powerful, so let it be said.

187. Fair One, the body must be known as made of the five Mahabhutas: the prithivi, the apas, the taijas, the vayu, and the akasa.

188. Bone, muscle, skin, Nadi and hair: these are the fivefold prithivi as laid down by the Brahmavidya [the divine science].

189. The semen, the female genital fluid, fat, urine and saliva: these are the fivefold apas as laid down by the Brahmavidya.

190. Hunger, thirst, sleep, light, drowsiness: these are the fivefold agni as laid down by the Brahmavidya.

191. Removing, walking, smelling, contraction and inflation: these are the fivefold vayu as laid down by the Brahmavidya.

192. Desire to have, desire to repel, shame, fear and forgetfulness: these are the fivefold akasa as laid down by the divine science.

193. The prithivi has five qualities, the apas four, the taijas three, the vayu two, the akasa one. This is a portion of tatwic knowledge.

194. The prithivi is 50 pala [pala = 1/3 ounce], the apas 40; the taijas 30; the vayu 20; the akasa 10.

195. In the prithivi income is delayed; in the apas it comes at once; in the vayu it is very little; in the agni even what is at hand is destroyed.

196. [The lunar mansions] (1) Dhanestha, (2) Rohini, (3) Jyestha, (4) Anaradha, (5) Srawana, (6) Abhiji, and (7) Uttarashadh: these are said to be the prithivi tatwa.

197. (1) Bharani, (2) Krithka, (3) Pushya, (4) Magha, (5) Purvaphalguni, (6) Purvabhadrapada, and (7) Swath: these are said to be the taijas tatwa.

198. (1) Purva shada, (2) Shelesha, (3) Mula, (4) Ardra, (5) Revati, (6) Uttara bhadrapada, and (7) Satabhisha: these are the apas tatwa, O Beloved!

199. (1) Vishakha, (2) Uttaragphalguni, (3) Hasta, (4) Chitra, (5) Punarvasu. (6) Ashwani, and (7) Mrigashirsha: these are the vayu tatwa.

200. Whatever good or bad the messenger asks about, standing towards the flowing Nadi, comes not to pass as he desires. In the empty Nadi it is the reverse.

201. Even when the Nadi is full, but the tatwa is not congenial, there is no success. The sun or the moon gives success only when combines with the congenial tatwa.

202. Rama got victory in an auspicious tatwa; so did Arjuna. The Kauravas were all killed in battle on account of the antagonistic tatwa.

203. By the acquired velocity of other births, or by the kindness of the guru, some men come to know the nature of the tatwas by a mind purified by habituation.

The Meditation of the Five Tatwas ~

204. Meditate upon the prithivi tatwa with L [or Lam] as its algebraic symbol, as being quadrangular, yellow, sweet-smelling, and conferring a color as pure as that of gold, freedom from disease and lightness of the body.

205. Mediate upon the apas tatwa with V [or Vam] as its algebraic sybol, as being semi- lunar, white as the moon, and giving endurance of hunger and thirst, etc., and producing a sensation similar to that of a plunge in water.

206. Meditate upon the taijas tatwa with R [or Ram] as the algebraic symbol, as being triangular, red, and giving the power of consuming a good deal of food and drink, and the endurance of burning heat.

207. Meditate upon the vayu tatwa with P [or Pam] as the algebraic symbol, as being spherical, sky-blue, and giving the power of going into the space, and flying like bird.

208. Meditate upon the akasa tatwa with H [or Ham] as the algebraic symbol, formless, foreshadowing many colors, and as giving the knowledge of the three times, and the powers Anima, etc.

209. Where there is a man who knows the science of breath, there can be no wealth better than him. It is known that by the Knowledge of breath one gets good fruit without much ado.

The Auspicious Victory ~

210. Great Lord! The god of gods, the giver of happiness, the science of the rise of breath is a very high science; how does it comprehend the Knowledge of the three times?

211. Said the god: Fair one! The knowledge of three times refers to three things, and nothing else: (1) Fortune, (2) Victory in battle, and (3) Good or bad [end of other actions].

212. On account of the tatwa any act is good or bad in effect; on account of the tatwa comes victory or discomfiture; on account of the tatwa comes scarcity and wealth. The tatwas are said to show themselves in these three states.

213. Said the goddess: Great Lord! The god of gods, the all-comprehending ocean of this world is the greatest friend and help-mate of men, he who causes the fulfillment of all his works?

214. Siva said: The Prana alone is the highest friend, the Prana is the greatest helpmate, Fair one! There is no friend better than Prana.

215. Said the goddess: How does the force of Prana stand in the body? What is the appearance of Prana in the body? How is the Prana known by the Yogi to be acting in the tatwas?

216. Siva said: In the city of the body the Prana is the Lord Protector; while going in, it is 10 fingers; while going out, 12.

Notes ~ This section refers to the human Aura. The subtle Prana surrounds the gross human body like a halo of light. The natural length from the body to the circumference of this halo is 12 fingers of the man whose Prana is measured. This length is affected during the ordinary course of inspiration and expiration. At the time of inspiration the length is reduced to 10 fingers; at the time of expiration it is restored to 12. During certain other actions too, the length varies. Thus, in walking the length of Prana becomes 24; in running, 42. In cohabitation it becomes 65; in sleeping, 100. In eating and speaking, it becomes 18. In ordinary men, the length is 12 fingers. The ordinary length is, however, reduced in extraordinary men. Thus, in those men who are free from desire, the length of Prana is reduced by one finger; it becomes 11. In men who are always pleasant, always hilarious, the length is 10 fingers. A poet has 9 fingers. A speaker has 8. A seer has s 7. A levitator has 6, and so on. See the following stanzas.

217. In walking it is 24 fingers, in running 42; in cohabitation 65; in sleeping 100 fingers.

218. The natural length of Prana, my goddess, is 12 fingers. In eating and speaking it stretches to 18 fingers.

219. When the Prana is reduced by one finger, freedom from desire is the result. Pleasure results when it is reduced by 2; poetical power when by 3;

220. Power of speech when by 4; second sight when by 5; levitation when by 6; great rapidity when by 7;

221. The eight siddhi when by 8; the nine niddhis when by 9; the ten figures when by 10, the loss of the shadow when by 11;

222. When it is reduced by 12 the inspiratory and expiratory motions

drink of the fountain of immortality at the sun [the center of Prana]. When the prana fills the body up to the end of nails even, for whom else then is food?

223. Thus has been described the law of prana. It can be known by the teaching of a guru, not by millions of sciences and shastra.

224. If the moon does not set in by chance in the morning, and the sun in the evening, they do so respectively after midday and midnight.

The Battle ~

225. In distant warfare the moon is victorious; in near places the sun. When the foot is raised first in going belongs to the flowing Nadi, complete success is the result.

226. In beginning a journey, in marriage, in entering any town, etc., in all auspicious acts, the flow of the moon is good.

227. Putting the enemy's army towards the empty Nadi, and one's own towards the full, when the tatwa is congenial, one might conquer the whole world.

228. Let one give battle in the direction towards which the breath flows; victory is certain, even if Indra is in front.

229. If a man puts a question about battle, he will win if he is towards the flowing Nadi,

230. The prithivi tatwa points to wounds in the belly, the apas in the feet; the agni in the thighs; the vayu in the hands.

231. The akasa in the head. These fivefold wounds have been described in the Science of Breath.

232. He whose name has even letters wins, if he asks the question during the flow of the moon. He who has an odd number of letters in his name wins if he asks the question during the flow of the sun.

233. When the question is put during the moon there will be a peaceful termination; during the sun the fight must come.

234. During the prithivi tatwa, the fight will be equal. During the apas the result will be equal. During the taijas there will be defeat. During the

vayu and the akasa death will ensue.

235. When by some cause the flow of the breath is not clearly felt at the time of the question, let the wise man resort to the following expedient;

236. Sitting motionless let him have a flower thrown upon himself. The flower will fall on the full side. So let him give the answer.

237. Here or elsewhere the knower of the laws of breath is very powerful; who is more powerful than he?

238. Said the goddess: These are the laws of victory when men fight among themselves; how does victory come when they fight with Yama [the god of death]?

239. Let him meditate upon the Lord when the prana is calm; during the flow of the moon and then give up life when after that the two pranas coincide. He will have what he desires: great benefit and success.

240. The whole unmanifested world has come out of the unmanifested. That manifested world disappears in the unmanifested when the fact is known.

How To Produce Sexual Attachment ~

241. Said the goddess: Great Lord! Thou hast given a description of the battle among men, and with Death; tell me now how to produce attachment between the sexes.

242. Said the god: It has been said by the Yogis that if one places himself in the sphere of prana, by drawing the moon with the sun, the female will be eternally attached.
Notes ~ The sphere of Prana means the halo of this force which surrounds the gross body. At the time when the male prana has the pure color of the sun, and the female that of the moon, let the two halos be brought together. They are at that moment in their own element. As the two halos come together, they all exchange color. With a certain amount of natural satisfaction the individual sun will contract the habit of being satisfied by the individual female prana, and vice versa. This must of course be repeated for some time in order to give each of the two pranas the permanent color of the other. One more thing must be done. Any antagonistic colors must not be allowed to take even the slightest hold of either of these pranas. If this is done the two will learn to repel each other, and instead of attachment enmity will result.

243. The prana is caught by the prana if the prana does give himself up. When the prana goes in the place of the prana, short life is destroyed.

Notes ~ The first and third pranas in the verse mean either the male or the female, while the second means the reverse of either. It means that the male or female prana takes with its substance the female or male prana, if either of the latter allow. This permission must have two phases. There must be a willing mind, otherwise an antagonistic color will be introduced and consequent repulsion.

There must also be an active throwing out of any antagonistic colors that might be present in the prana, and also a shutting up of both mind and prana against any antagonistic influences.

When the male or female prana goes in the place of, i.e., is saturated in the female or male prana, life is at an end. The negative prana gives general strength to positive and vice versa. Strength causes long life. But in order to receive length of life there must be a complete saturation, which is impossible with the presence in any one of these pranas of any other antagonistic prana.

244 –249. ---

250. When in the beginning of the monthly period the males have the sun and the females the moon, even the barren woman gets a child.

251. In questions about the result of a pregnancy, a female child is born if the moon be flowing; a male during the flow of the sun. If both are flowing, the fetus will be destroyed.

252. At the time of this question, when the messenger is towards the moon, a female child is born; when towards the sun, a male child; when in the middle, a hermaphrodite. When he is towards the full Nadi a son is born.

253. The prithivi brings a son; the apas a son; in vayu comes a girl; in the taijas the fetus is destroyed; the akasa brings a hermaphrodite.

254. When the nostril is empty, nothing is born; when two tatwas join, twins are born. When one is passing into another, the fetus is destroyed. When this happens during the flow of the moon, the result is a female child; when the sun, a male.

255. During the vishuvu conjunction the fetus is destroyed, or a hermaphrodite is born. Fair One! I tell thee, the knower of the tatwas can know all this.

256. When at the time of conception the vayu tatwa flows, the child will be a sufferer; when the apas tatwa flows, the child will be happy and renowned. When the taijas tatwa flows, the fetus is destroyed, or the child is short-lived. When the prithivi tatwa flows, the child is wealthy and full of enjoyment.

257. During the apas tatwa the child that is conceived is always wealthy, happy, and full of enjoyment. During the akasa the fetus is destroyed.

258. During the prithivi a son is born, during the apas a girl. During other tatwas either the fetus is destroyed or the child is short-lived.

Notes ~ These two stanzas (253, 258) seem at first sight to record different truths. But they refer to different pranas: the one to the positive, the other to the negative.

This can be easily known from a teacher, not by millions of sciences and shastras.

Notes ~ The female cells in the ovary are the moon. They have the capability of being impressed into any form by the male cells, the sun. The semen is hotter than the germ cells of the female. As the former act upon the latter, these expand. The former only act upon the latter when these present themselves to them; this is expressed by saying that the sun enters the moon, and the moon enters the sun. When both of these thus enter each other, the female matter that receives constant nourishment by the help of the Power KundAlini begins to expand along the lines stretched for it by the inherent power of the sun. In the semen lies hidden the future man, just as a tree in the seed. This is a veritable picture of the sun, or we might say a macrocosmic prana. The semen virile is, in fact, the mirror in which on account of tatwic affinity is reflected the individual truti, with which the reader must now be familiar. The semen thus is the reservoir of the whole pranamaya Kosha.

The Year ~

260. On the first lunar day of the white fortnight of the month of Chaitra, let the wise yogi see both the northward and southward journey of the sun by an analysis of the tatwas.

Notes ~ On this day begins the sanwat year of the era of King Vikramaditya.

261. If at the time of the rise of the moon, the prithivi, the apas, or the vayu taTwa is flowing, all kinds of grain will be plentiful.

262. The flow of the taijas and the akasa gives fearful famines. This is the nature of Time. In this way is known the effect of Time in the year, the month, and the day.

263. If the susumna, which is bad in all worldly concerns, is flowing, there will be confusion in the land, subversion of the kingdom, or fear thereof, epidemic, and all sorts of diseases.

264. When the sun passes into Aries, let the yogi meditate upon the breath and, finding out the prevalent tatwa, tell the world what will be the nature of the next year.

Notes ~ On this day the solar year begins. The tatwic color of the Universal Prana, the External one, is determined at any time by the positions of the sun and moon and by those of the planets, whose presence exercises a very potent influence upon the tatwic value of any moment. This tatwic value changes according to a universal law.

If at any time the apas tatwa is flowing, it can never abruptly change into the taijas, but must do so grade by grade. These atmospheric taijas run many minor courses. Hence it is possible, though extremely difficult and complicated, to calculate from the tatwic value of one moment the tatwic value of any future moment.

The living world is always affected by these tatwic changes. In the act of breathing nature has furnished a very exact and faithful scale for the measurement of tatwic changes. Hence the yogi, who can live in conformity with time and space, can foretell the future very easily. Ah! But how very difficult it is to live in perfect harmony with time and space!

265. The good aspect of the year, the month, and the day is known by the tatwas, prithivi, etc., and the bad one by the akasa and the vayu.

266. If the prithivi tatwa flows there will be plenty and prosperity in the kingdom, and the earth will be full of good crops; there will be much comfort and enjoyment.

267. If the apas tatwa flows there will be plenty of rain, plenty of grain, great comfort, and well-grown fields.

268. If the agni tatwa flows there will be famine, subversion, or fear thereof; there will be fearful epidemics and the least possible rain.

269. If the vayu tatwa flows when the sun goes into Aries, there will be confusion, accidents, famine, little rain, or the itis [six afflictions that distress crops: too much rain, etc.].

270. If the akasa tatwa flows when the sun goes into Aries, there will be want of grain and comfort.

271. When the full breath is in its own proper place, with its own proper tatwa, success of all sorts is the result. If the sun and the moon are the reverse, grain must be laid up [against a scarcity].

272. If the agni tatwa flows there will be inequality of prices; if akasa, there will be continuous scarcity. Let things be laid up then; there will be a rise in the prices two months thereafter.

273. When the breath is changing into the sun it gives birth to fearful diseases. When the
akasa and the vayu are conjoined with the taijas, the earth will become the picture of hell.

Notes ~ The disturbance of tatwic balance is disease; hence every tatwa has its own diseases.

The Diseased ~

274. In the prithivi tatwa there is its own disease; in the apas the disease of the same tatwa; and so in the taijas, the vayu, and the akasa, similar and hereditary diseases.

Notes ~ When two men come together their pranas exchange color. It is on this account that you can measure from the momentary reflection in your own body the color of any other man that is near you. The present of every man is the father of is future. Hence you can predict the end of any disease, or the time of death.

All that has been ascertained to be true on these heads has been described in the various sections of this book.

The "messenger" in 275 is the man who comes to ask questions about anything.

275. When the messenger comes first towards the empty half of the body, and then towards the full half, he about whom the question is put will surely live, even if he is [apparently] lying in the swoon [of death].

276. If the question is put to the yogi while sitting in the same direction with the patient, he will live even though many a disease might have gathered strength in his body.

277. When the breath is in the right nostril, and the messenger speaks of his afflictions in piteous accents, the patient will live.

278. If the question is asked while holding the picture of the patient towards the prana and looking at it, the patient will live.

279. When during the flow of the sun or the moon, the yogi gets into a carriage and the question is put to him while there, the message will have success in his desire.

280. When at the time of the question the yogi sits upstairs while the patient is downstairs, he will certainly live. If the patient is upstairs, he will certainly go to the house of Yama [the god of death].

281. If at the time of the question the messenger is towards the empty nostril, he will have success. If the reverse is the case, the result too is the reverse.

282. When the patient is towards the moon and the asker towards the sun the patient will certainly die, even if he is surrounded by hundreds of physicians.

283. When the patient is towards the sun, and the asker towards the moon, then too the patient dies, even if Sambhu be his protector.

284. When one tatwa is out of its proper time, people are subdued by disease; when two are wrong, they cause misfortune to friends and relation; if it is out of place for two fortnights death is the result.

The Prediction of Death ~

285. In the beginning of a month, a fortnight, and a year, let the wise man try to find out the time of death from the movements of prana.

286. The lamp of the five tatwas receives its oil from the moon. Protect it from the solar fire; life will thereby become long and stationary.

287. If by mastering the flow of breath, the sun is kept in check, life is prolonged. Even solar time is cheated.

288. The moon falls from heaven giving the nectar of life to the lotuses of the body. By the constant practice of good actions and yoga one becomes immortal by the lunar nectar.

289. Make the sun flow during the day, the sun during the night. He who practices thus is doubtless a true yogi.

290. If for one night and day continuously the breath flows in one

Nadi, full three years will bring death.

291. He whose breath flows by the Pingala two whole days and nights continuously has, as the knowers of the tatwas say, two years more to live.

292. If the moon flows continuously during the night and the sun during the day, death will come within six months.

293. When the sun flows altogether, and the moon is not altogether seen, death comes by a fortnight. So says the science of death.

294. He whose breath flows from one nostril for three nights continuously has, so say the wise, a year only to live.

295. Take a vessel of the Kansya alloy. Fill it with water, and see in it the reflection of the sun. If in the midst of the reflection is seen a hole, the seer will die within ten days. If the reflection is smoky, death will come the same day. If it is seen towards the south, West and North respectively, death will come within six, two and three months. Thus has been described the measure of life by the omniscient.

296. [If a man sees the figure of the messengers of death he is sure to die]. The messenger of death has red or reddish clothes, matted hair, diseased teeth, oil-besmeared body, a weeping and red-hot face, a body besmeared with ashes, flying flames of fire, having heavy long rods, and standing towards the empty Nadi.

297. When the skin is cool but the inside is hot, death must come within a month.

298. When a man changes suddenly and unaccountably from good habits to bad, or from bad habits to good, he is sure to die.

299. He whose breath that comes out of the nose is cool, but that which comes out of the mouth is hot like fire, is sure to die of great heat.

300. He who sees hideous figures, and bright light without making out the flame, lives not for nine months.

301. He who suddenly begins to feel heavy bodies light, and light bodies heavy, and he who being dark in color begins in disease to look gold-colored, must die!

302. He whose hands, chest, and feet become at once dry after bathing has not ten nights to live.

303. He who becomes dim of sight, and cannot see his face in the pupil of another's eye must doubtless die.

304. Now I shall tell thee something about the shady Figure [Chya Purusha]. Knowing this, man very soon becomes the knower of the three times.

305. I shall speak of those experiments by means of which even distant death is known. I shall describe all these in accordance with the Sivagama.

306. Going to a lonely place and standing with the back towards the sun let a man look with attention into the neck of the shade he throws on the ground.

307. Let him see this for as long a time as he can calmly repeat the words: "Om Kram parabrahman namah" for 108 times. Then let him look up into the sky. He will thus see Shankara [the figure of a being capable of appearing in many colors].

308. By doing this for six months, the yogi becomes the lord of those who walk on earth; by two years he becomes absolutely independent and his own master.

309. He obtains the knowledge of the three times and great bliss. There is nothing impossible for the constant practice of Yoga.

310. The Yogi who sees this figure in the clear heavens having a dark color, dies within six months.

311. When it is yellow there is fear of disease; when it is red there will be loss; when it has many colors there will be great confusion and dejection.

312. If the figure be wanting in feet, shanks, abdomen and the right arm, a relation is sure to die.

313. If the left arm is wanting, the wife will die; when the chest and the right arm is wanting, death and destruction will come.

314. When the feces and gas escape at once, the man is sure to die in ten days.

315. When the moon flows altogether, and the sun is not seen at all, death comes surely within a month.

316. Those whose death is near cease to see the Arandhati, the Druhva, the steps of Vishnu, and the circle of the mothers as they are pointed out to them.

317. The Arundhati is the tongue; the Dhruva the tip of the nose; the eyebrows are the steps of Vishnu; the pupil of the eye is the circle of the mothers.

318. The man who ceases to see the eyebrows dies within nine days; he who ceases to see the pupil of the eye dies within five days; he who ceases to see the nose dies within three days; he who ceases to see the tongue dies within one day.

319. The pupil of the eye is seen by pressing the eye near the nose.

The Nadis ~

320 The Ida is also technically called Ganga; the Pingala, Yamuna; the Susumna, Saraswati; the conjunction is called Prayaga.

321. Let the Yogi sit in the posture called padmasana, and perform pranayama.

322. The Yogi must know the puraka, the rechaka, and the third Kumbhaka for obtaining power over the body.

323. The puraka causes growth and nourishment, and equalizes the humors; the Kumbhaka causes stability, and increases the security of life.

324. The Rechaka takes away all the sins. He who practices this reaches the state of yoga.

325. In the Kumbhaka hold the air in as much as possible; let it go out by the moon and in by the sun.

326. The sun drinks the moon, the moon drinks the sun; by saturating one with the other, one may live till the moon and the planets.

327. The Nadi flows in one's own body. Have power over that; if it is not let go through the mouth or nose, one becomes a young man.

328. When the mouth, nose, eyes and ears are stopped by the fingers, the tatwas begin to take their rise before the eyes.

329. He who knows their color, their motion, their taste, their places, and their signs, becomes in this world equal to the god Rudra.

330. He who knows all this, and reads it always, is freed from all pain and gets what he desires.

331. He who has the knowledge of breath in his head, has fortune at his feet.

332. Like the One in the Vedas, and the sun in the Universe, is the knower of the Science of Breath to be honored. He who knows the Science of Breath and the Philosophy of the Tatwas, knows not even millions of elixirs to be equal to it.

333. There is nothing in the world that will release you of the debt of the man who gives you the knowledge of the word [Om] and of breath.

334. Sitting in his own place, with measured food, and sleep, let the Yogi meditate upon the highest Atma [whose reflection the Breath is]. Whatever he says will come to pass.

The End.

www.ingramcontent.com/pod-product-compliance
Lightning Source LLC
Chambersburg PA
CBHW070835100426
42813CB00003B/628